Housemates Returns

Is Dat U Yh?

dkfash

Before I Go

Tobi King Bakare

T0019094

methuen | drama

LONDON · NEW YORK · OXFORD · NEW DELHI · SYDNEY

METHUEN DRAMA
Bloomsbury Publishing Plc
50 Bedford Square, London, WC1B 3DP, UK
1385 Broadway, New York, NY 10018, USA
29 Earlsfort Terrace, Dublin 2, Ireland

BLOOMSBURY, METHUEN DRAMA and the Methuen
Drama logo are trademarks of Bloomsbury Publishing Plc

First published in Great Britain 2024

Is Dat U Yh? copyright © dkfash, 2024

Before I Go copyright © Tobi King Bakare, 2024

dkfash and Tobi King Bakare have asserted their rights
under the Copyright, Designs and Patents Act, 1988, to be
identified as authors of this work.

Cover images: *Is Dat U Yh?* illustration by Ali 'Komikamo' Kamara;
Before I Go cover image © The Other Richards

All rights reserved. No part of this publication may be reproduced or
transmitted in any form or by any means, electronic or mechanical, including
photocopying, recording, or any information storage or retrieval system,
without prior permission in writing from the publishers.

Bloomsbury Publishing Plc does not have any control over, or responsibility
for, any third-party websites referred to or in this book. All internet addresses
given in this book were correct at the time of going to press. The author and
publisher regret any inconvenience caused if addresses have changed or sites
have ceased to exist, but can accept no responsibility for any such changes.

No rights in incidental music or songs contained in the work are hereby
granted and performance rights for any performance/presentation
whatsoever must be obtained from the respective copyright owners.

All rights whatsoever in these plays are strictly reserved and application
for performance etc. should be made before rehearsals by professionals
and by amateurs to Permissions Department, Methuen Drama,
Bloomsbury Publishing Plc, 50 Bedford Square, London
WC1B 3DP Performance.Permissions@bloomsbury.com.
No performance may be given unless a licence has been obtained.

A catalogue record for this book is available from the British Library.

Library of Congress Control Number: 2024935287

ISBN: PB: 978-1-3505-1081-4
ePDF: 978-1-3505-1082-1
eBook: 978-1-3505-1083-8

Series: Modern Plays

Typeset by Mark Heslington Ltd, Scarborough, North Yorkshire

To find out more about our authors and books visit
www.bloomsbury.com and sign up for our newsletters.

Brixton House

Brixton House is a new cultural space, developed from the rich and influential history of Ovalhouse Theatre, which presents and collaborates with voices and perspectives not currently centered in mainstream culture. We focus on theatrical stories told through theatre and multiple other art forms.

Located in the heart of Brixton, South London, we are a home for artists and a new generation of makers, artists, writers, producers, technicians and audiences, curating new experiences that develop community solidarity and passion for social change. Continuing our legacy of championing innovation and creative expression, Brixton House presents work that is rich in stories that resonate with its local, international, and intergenerational communities. We are committed to, and representative of Brixton, where the lively and diverse communities who live, work and come together to engage with culture and build community.

Our vision is to empower our undervalued, unheard, and excluded communities through our creative and cultural spaces.

Our House is a space where people come together, to create and enjoy performances. We have two studio theatres, performance spaces, seven rehearsal rooms and multi-use meeting rooms, as well as public spaces, a café and a bar. Brixton House is generously supported by the London Borough of Lambeth, Arts Council England, Garfield Weston Foundation, the Wolfson Foundation, Cockayne Grants for the Arts, London Community Fund, and the 29th May 1961 Charitable Trust.

Brixton House Team

Managing Director   Delia Barker

Executive Director   Gary Johnson

Head of Finance   Yaw Manu

Finance Officer   Adeshola Wusu

**Head of Programming and
Producing**   Ruth Hawkins
Producer   Ben Quashie

**Head of Communications
and Audience Development**   Monique Baptiste-Brown

**Box Office & Ticketing
Coordinator**   Liam Purshouse

Box Office Assistant   Paxina Tuvuka

Marketing Manager   Charley Strachan

**Freelance Marketing
Manager**   Holly Adomah

**Digital Marketing
Coordinators**   Jade Bellevue de Sylva
Toyin Dawudu

**Head of Technical,
Production & Building
Services**   Richard Owen

Senior Technician   Nevi Kusokora

Technicians   Henry Boothroyd
Eve Shalmon

Event Technicians   Niall Rowley
Tem Uwawah

Maintenance Technician   Erik Keen

Head of Creative Engagement	Michelle McGrath
Creative Engagement Producer	Nina Graveney-Edwards
Demonstrate! Project Manager	Nicola Rayworth
Head of Commercial and Operations	Sika Tro
Operations Manager	Lili-Mae Billam
Venue Duty Managers	Nadir Rahman, Rebekka Absolon, Sade Byfield-Crouch
Tenant & Space Hire Coordinator	Lina Ruales

Brixton House Front of House Team

Dirg Aaab-Richards, Elsie Yager, Emanuel Vuso, Hajar Mounamak, Kimberley N'doueyo, Bridge, Niyah Lee-Edwards, Jack Sadhu, Kenza Hameddine, Nesmie Constantine, Amabel Cofie, Aziza Brown, Bufweme Pongolati, Ian Marciano, Kaiya Koroma, Lia-Maria Popescu, Lola Smith, Aderly Gonzalez, Niamh James, Niyah Lee-Edwards, Nora Azmani, Ryan Romin, Salha Jamal, Zak Shetewi

Brixton House Board Members

(Chair) David Bryan, Eddy Akang, Richard Beecham, Sunil Chotai, Maya Groves, Fionnuala Hogan, Christina Liciaga, Abbie Agana, Jacqui Beckford and Carole Stewart

Brixton House Housemates Festival

Brixton House, formerly Ovalhouse, has a long legacy of supporting early career to established artists to have the freedom and space to playfully experiment, explore ideation and tell stories from their own nuanced perspectives. Since opening the doors to our home in Brixton, we have continued this commitment with the launch of the Housemates Festival.

The Housemates Festival leads with an open call out for ideas, scripts and creative ideas across genres and forms that speak to our vision of empowering undervalued, unheard, and excluded communities through creative and cultural work. Now in its third year, Housemates has worked with over 35 companies and many more individual artists since launching in 2022 and has supported the creative ambitions of new work to be presented on stage exploring the intersections, cultures and lived experiences in Brixton and further afield.

The Housemates Festival runs annually and invites artists locally, nationally, and internationally to share their stories. Each year we commit to bringing at least one show back from the Festival for a further run, ensuring we are working to support the development of artists.

BRIXTON HOUSE

SEP 24 - OCT 24

Housemates Festival 2024

Housemates Festival is back for 2024 championing work from artists telling stories from their lived experiences. Prepare for a 3-week artist takeover of our House!

The full programme and tickets go on sale July 2024. Join our mailing list for the latest updates.

brixtonhouse.co.uk
020 7582 7680

 @brxhousetheatre

Initiative.dkf

Initiative.dkf is an independent award-winning multidisciplinary arts duo. They produce theatre, dance events, festivals and cultivate culture through instinctual and interdisciplinary work. Exploring without limitation, and birthing the imaginary on stage, screen and all in-between. Led by Artistic Director dkfash and Creative Producer Wofai. Creators of Melanin Box Festival (UK's first festival dedicated to spotlighting the work of Black British creatives through theatre, short film, monologues and live PAs); outdoor spectacle *Scalped* (Without Walls, UK Tour); short films collection LUDALA (Edinburgh Fringe on demand); and three-part miniseries *Afrodance Talk* (The Space). They are winners of the Eclipse Award '21, Albany Theatre Artists of Change '21, Tamasha Associate Co. '19/20 and Talawa MAKE: Artists '17.

Is Dat U Yh?
dkfash (**Writer and Director**)

dkfash is an interdisciplinary artist working across stage, film and entertainment. Her instinctual practice explores storytelling; through text, physical theatre, chorus, surrealism and collaborative devising.

Writer and director: Brixton House (*Is Dat U Yh?*); Theatre503 (*Fragments of a Complicated Mind*); Without Walls national tour (*Scalped*). Movement includes: Sheffield Theatres, Unicorn Theatre, Royal Shakespeare Company, Bush Theatre, Royal Exchange Manchester, Talawa and National Youth Theatre.

A range of other work includes the UK premiere of *Bootycandy* (Gate Theatre; Offie nomination Best Ensemble), choreography for *Wizkid* (Zinarts) and twerk artist for legendary Big Freedia.

Wofai (**Initiative.dkf: Executive Producer**)

LTC × MOBOs Fellow 2023 and Stage ONE Bursary Recipient, Wofai is a Creative and Executive Producer, an established model, and sometimes poet.

With a focus on executive acumen, bid writing and script dissection, he is passionate about interdisciplinary projects that push boundaries and challenge societal norms. After taking part in Young Vic's Introduction to Directing Programs (2016) he was hand-picked for their Springboard scheme.

Other experience includes: *The Blu Palace Ball* (Bishopsgate × Guildhall); *Dear Elizabeth '22* (Gate Theatre @ Teatro Technis); Part of the Main '19; China Plate Optimists '17; AD @ VAULT Festival '17; UpShot #50Uprise (*From Behind Us*).

Roisin Jenner (**Set and Costume Designer**)

Roisin Jenner is a set and costume designer for theatre and a set and production designer for music and fashion. Her recent credits for theatre include: *Karen* (The Other Place/Tour); *Henry V* schools' tour (Donmar Warehouse); *What the Heart Wants* (Hen and Chickens/

Tour); *Essentially Black* (Soho Theatre); *Jane Eyre* (Minack Theatre); *Contact* (Golden Goose); *Footmonster, Please Hold* (Actors East); *The Wedding, 4.48 Psychosis* (LIPA).

Xana (Sound Designer)

XANA is a freestyle live loop musician, composer, spatial sound artist, music supervisor and a haptic specialist sound designer developing accessible audio systems for live art spaces. XANA is the music science and technology lead and project mentor supporting artists and inventors at audio research label Inventing Waves.

Theatre credits include: *Elephant, Sleepova, The P Word, Shifters, Strange Fruit* (Bush); *The Architect* (ATC/GDIF); *Beautiful Thing* (Stratford East); *Imposter 22, Word:Play, Living Newspaper #4* (Royal Court); *Rumble In the Jungle* (Rematch:Live); *Anna Karerina* (Edinburgh Lyceum, Bristol Old Vic); *Galatea* (Wildworks); *The Trials, Mary Seacole* (Donmar Warehouse); *Earthworks, Sundown Kiki: Reloaded, The Collaboration, Sundown Kiki, Changing Destiny, Fairview, Ivan and the Dogs* (Young Vic); *…cake* (Theatre Peckham); *Who Killed My Father* (Tron); *as british as a watermelon* (Contact); *Hyde and Seek* (Guildhall); *Burgerz* (Hackney Showroom); *Everyday* (Deafinitely); *Black Holes* (The Place); *Sankofa: Before the Whitewash, Hive City Legacy* (Roundhouse); *Glamrou: From Quran to Queen, Curious, Half-Breed* (Soho); *Blood Knot* (Orange Tree); *Samuel Takes A Break, SEX SEX MEN MEN* (Yard); *Everything I Own* (Brixton House).

Winner of Olivier Award for Outstanding Achievement in an Affiliate Theatre 2023 for *The P Word* and Best Sound Design at Black British Theatre Awards 2023; finalist for sound design Offie for *Sleepova, The P Word* and *Blood Knot*; nominated for Olivier Award for Outstanding Achievement in Affiliate Theatre 2024 for *Sleepova*.

Jahmiko Marshall (Lighting Designer)

Jahmiko Marshall is a Lighting and Sound Designer from Bermuda.

He obtained his Lighting Technology Certificate from Stagecraft Institute of Las Vegas. He is currently a student at LAMDA studying towards his BA Hons in Production and Technical Arts. Before arriving in London, Jahmiko was heavily involved in light design for all the productions at his high school in Bermuda which is where he developed his passion for theatre.

Recent credits include, as sound designer: *Parliament Square*, *Desert Boy*, *The Light* (LAMDA); as assistant sound designer: *For Black Boys Who Have Considered Suicide When The Hue Gets Too Heavy* (New Diorama/Royal Court); as Chief LX: *Spalding Suite*, *Love and Information* (LAMDA); as lighting designer, *Against* and *The Welkin* (LAMDA); as assistant lighting designer: *Boy* (LAMDA); as programmer: *Junkyard* (LAMDA).

Trybe House Theatre

Trybe House Theatre (THT) is a company that primarily focus on supporting young black men by actively building resilience and well-being through theatre.

The team consists of Artistic Director Philip J Morris, Creative Producer Chenube-Ruth Bailey, Wellbeing Lead Stefan Livingston and Associate Director David Gilbert.

THT engages in interactive workshops designed to facilitate emotional understanding and trust, encouraging openness, and sharing, and developing a sense of purpose and connectivity.

Recognizing the alarming statistics on the disparity between black men seeking help and accessing support, THT aims to fill this gap by providing a space where young men can express themselves. The company creates work that reflects the lived experiences of the men they work with and encourages them to tell their stories unapologetically. This approach is crucial in addressing the mental health needs of young black men.

After a successful pilot launch in 2021, the company has grown rapidly, providing a platform serves young black men across the four corners of London. THT have partnered with some of London's notable theatres, ranging from the National Theatre, National Youth Theatre, and the Royal Court Theatre.

Before I Go

Tobi King Bakare (Writer)

Tobi King Bakare trained at RAaW in Southwark, London. Tobi is an actor and writer, most known for *Temple* seasons 1 and 2 (Sky One) starring as Jamie, *Cursed* (Netflix) and *I May Destroy You* (BBC1). He was recently seen in *Marriage* (BBC).

His most recent stage work includes *For Black Boys...* in the West End and his own one-man play *Before I Go* (Peckham Theatre/Camden People's Theatre). The show jumps beautifully between verse and prose, focussing on how to express yourself within the many barriers one might face. He also performed in Camden People's Theatre's *Fog Everywhere*.

Most recently he has led the short film *Non Recyclables*, directed by upcoming writer/director Jake Kuhn, and was seen in the feature film *Cerebrum* directed by Sebastian Blanc.

Trybe House Theatre (Co-producer for Before I Go)

Trybe House Theatre (THT) is an enterprise that seeks to actively build resilience and self-wellbeing, primarily with young black men aged 16–25, using theatre as a supportive outlet

Chenube-Ruth Bailey (Creative Producer for Trybe House)

Chenube-Ruth Bailey is the Creative Producer at Trybe House Theatre, blending her passion for theatre with community engagement. Following her Musical Theatre diploma, she transitioned to behind-the-scenes roles, orchestrating events like the Lewisham Live Festival at Trinity Laban and spearheading projects at Greenwich Dance. Alongside, she delved into casting for Film/TV and Musical Theatre, with credits including *Crazy For You* (Chichester Festival Theatre) and *Breathtaking* (ITV).

At Trybe House Theatre, Chenube-Ruth leads a team dedicated to supporting young black men's mental well-being through theatre. Her journey reflects a deep appreciation for the arts and a commitment to amplifying community voices. Credits include *SWIM* (National Theatre Public Acts) and *TRYBE x NYT* (National Youth Theatre).

Chenube-Ruth's experiences reaffirm her belief in the transformative power of the arts, driving her to foster connections, artistic excellence, and positive change.

Philip J Morris (Artistic Director for Trybe House)

Philip J Morris is a London-born theatre director and practitioner raised in the borough of Croydon. He has directed plays regionally and internationally, working with professional actors, students, community groups and young people.

Philip received training at the Young Vic's Introduction to Directing course, Regional Theatre Young Directors' scheme RTYDS and became a Project Associate at the National Theatre for NT Public Acts. Following a period as Trainee Director at the Royal Court Theatre, he became the Artistic Director of Trybe House Theatre.

Theatre directing includes: *Romeo & Juliet, First Encounters* (Royal Shakespeare Company); *What I Hear I Keep,* TYPT Programme (Talawa); *Manorism*, an adaptation by Yomi Ṣode (Southbank Centre); *Bitches* (Residenz Theatre, Munich); *Of the Cut* (Young Vic); *Clutch* (Bush Theatre); *Sessions* (Paines Plough & Soho Theatre); *18, Company Three* (New Diorama Theatre); *Neighbourhood Voices Monologue Showcase* (Young Vic Theatre).

Film directing includes: *Recovery In Vision Short Films* (Tea Films & Outside Edge); *Living Newspaper Editions 4 & 7* (Royal Court Theatre).

Audio play credits include: *Copper & Lead* by Lydia Luke (Talawa & Radio 4); *The Holding 'GNR8' – Bad Seed* (LAMDA & Audible Original).

Stefan Livingston (Wellbeing Lead for Trybe House)

Stefan is the Wellbeing Lead at Trybe House Theatre. After receiving a degree in psychology, Stefan spent time working with Camden and Islington Youth Offending Services working as a wellbeing specialist. He then worked as a lead specialist practitioner at Catch-22 and Merton Children's Service, delivering support across three strands of specialist services, namely Missing Children, Child Exploitation and Drug and Alcohol Misuse. His passion took him on to working at Surrey Child and Adolescent Mental Health Services (CAMHS) within the Specialist Services. Stefan's experience compelled him to work closely with marginalised and underserved communities.

This production of *Is Dat U Yh?* was first performed on 17 April 2024 at Brixton House, London, with the following cast and creative team:

Debz	Adeola Yemitan
Tolu	Antonia Layiwola
Reena	Rachael Ridley
Tia	Zakiyyah Deen

Director and Movement	dkfash
Writer	dkfash
Set and Costume Designer	Roisin Jenner
Sound Designer	Xana
Original Sound Designer	Melo Zed
Lighting Designer	Jahmiko Marshall
Rehearsal Stage Manager	Tamasin Cook
Stage Manager	Chloe Astleford
Slang Song	Sir Loui
Scenic Painter	Jaida Salmon
Set Illustration	Wofai
Set Fabricator	Rusty Nutt Metalworks
Executive Producer for Initiative.dkf	Wofai
Dance Captain	Rachael Ridley

It was previously performed at the 2023 Housemates Festival (cast: Adeola Yemitan, Antonia Layiwola, Rujenne Green, Toyin Ayedun-Alase) and commissioned for outdoor at the 2021 Greenwich + Docklands International Festival and Albany Theatre (original devising cast: Antonia Layiwola, Effie Ansah, Rachael Ridley, Zakiyyah Deen).

This production of *Before I Go* will be performed from 15 July 2024 at Brixton House, London. At the time of publication, the cast and creative team were confirmed as follows:

Ajani

Tobi King Bakare, Christopher Mbaki

Writer	Tobi King Bakare
Director	Philip Morris
Casting Director	Chenube-Ruth Bailey
Wellbeing Lead for Trybe House Theatre	Stefan Livingstone
Creative Producer for Trybe House Theatre	Chenube-Ruth Bailey

Original Creative Team

Writer and Performer	Tobi King Bakare
Saxophonist	Lewis Daniel
Drummer	Tobi Adewumi
Director	Ozioma Ihesiene
Producer	Amaarah Roze
Movement Director	Aruken
Lighting Designer	Ezra Mortimer
Stage Manager	Justin Treadwell

Is Dat U Yh?

Teenage girlhood memories personified
A surreal adventure down memory lane
Love letters to a time when laughter was free

A thank you to a time that once was, and the people and communities who birthed them. To every class of 2005, to Jubz, Panda, Phebz, Gozi, Tolu, Rockstar.

To Mum for getting me the camcorder I begged for.

To Effie and Toni for sharing your memories

ORIGINALLY WRITTEN FOR FILM AS PART OF *LUDALA COLLECTION* BY INITIATIVE.DKF WHICH DEBUTED ON DEMAND THROUGH EDINBURGH FRINGE 2021 SUMMERHALL FESTIVAL FRINGE.

FINAL ACT 'THIS IS THAT' ORIGINALLY PERFORMED AS PART OF *ALL THE THINGS* AT ARTS ED 2021 BY DK FASHOLA

Performers

Tia aka Tia ('Lady 7')
Tolu aka Moodz
Deborah aka Debz
Reena aka Lady Savage

4+ (ensemble piece)
Cast/ensemble to play all extra roles

Text

anything in **bold** is to be said in chorus
unallocated lines to be decided in the room
/ = interruption from following line
// = interruptions from following first and second lines
simultaneously
all text in sans serif should lean into melody of some sort,
including lyrical flow, singing, rap, MC'ing and or
beatboxing influenced by African/Caribbean/AAVE cultural
styles – can also be presented through audio

PORTAL FLASH: a gentle sound | story/memory shifters,
causes quick sharp head pains and/or chest tightening

Note

Laughter hasn't been written in as you'll find it . . . and I'd
get tired of writing it.
There's no anger in this play; love and raw passion only.
Improvising is key for authenticity, we don't listen silently.
Through ad libbing utilise Black British dialects: Jamaican
Patois, Nigerian Pidgin

Set, Props, Lighting

everything is imaginable

Costume and Hair

pay homage to iconic styles and relevant fashion sense of teenagers/young adults in the late nineties to mid-noughties (forehead slick-down ponytails, Brandy burnt-end box braids, peacock updos, side part weaves)

Music/Sound

Old skool noughties mix of 'Black British culture' classics. With an imaginative and futuristic spin – the sound is an additional performer through ongoing soundlibs and soundbites. Unallocated lines can also be explored through audio/voiceovers. [ARTIST] in square brackets refers to specific musicality/flow of artists across the nineties/noughties.

'Pop ur bubble' in Hit Up Narm scene is influenced by UK grime artists. Penned by dkfash and Luke Wilson.

Enjoyment isn't free.

An adulting fever dream nightmare.
Reflection (R), Exhaustion (E), Regret (Reg), Bitterness (B) and
Hope (H) are entangled and magnified. Bodies weighted by the
corruption of adulthood and splintered by the manipulation of social
constructs.

Actions.times.actions.time.

R   In real time. A gift and a curse . . . Choices?

You see this life?
It's a labyrinth
Every part of our choices are made for us by a
greater architect they say
Soooo great that we believe we're part of the
building!
How can one be a thing yet be crafting that same
very thing?
We're alive, human, yes but what builds our
humanity?
Who sets the perception, the lens?
Morals vs anarchy?
Is it all really instinctual? Free will?
Or scientifically proven that a certain
environment, place and people
generate a certain . . . product?
I'm just chatting shit . . .
You see this life yh?
The older I get the less I know
So much unlearning, relearning without a crutch
Everything done has been un-done

Growing pains

E   I don't know about you, but me yh
Sometimes I get soooo exhausted
Time keeps going and I can't catch it and . . .
I just wanna chiiiill – without the tax

Sleeping in adulthood isn't free
Guilt tax . . . will find you
Oh when you think you can close one eyelid
Remove your lashes and sleep peacefully

Guilt tax. It follows me everywhere
Just one more hour in bed **Guilt tax**.
   you have to consider traffic
Just one night out **Guilt tax**.
   you have that deadline to make
Just one more drink **Guilt tax**.
   put that rum n coke down! did you not see the gas
   bill?
A karmic reminder of why your parents would
cuss you out if the lights were on during the day

Reg   *'Your chest is too high, relazz'*
Fine. You were right, Dad!
I know you're up there or down . . . hmph
well you're somewhere, with your arms extended

Imitates

palms out, eyebrow raised, with that exact
expression you make
Saying *'can you see yourself?'*
   'Slaving away without true gain ah ah!'

Smiling into regret

We had an argument a few weeks before he
passed.

He said this day would come
stubbornness clogged my ears at the . . .
You think there's **time** but there isn't
You can't hold time
So you *have* to cherish every minute
You can't fight time
It'll out run you every time.
To know then what I know now

B   Enjoyment. isn't. free.
Adulting = fully understanding that *you* have to
get *YOU* out of bed now.
No one is coming to save you.
      Suck it up!
We all wanted to grow up so bad
Not knowing these adult privileges come with
endless bandages
This can't be it?
'Cause living to survive? is torment
What's the point in putting in work
without h'enjoyment?
But that guilt tax is real
Back and forth
But it won't follow you to the grave?
back and forth
nothing does so . . .

Moesha diary theme

H   Take your time appreciate each moment
Aiming for the stars doesn't mean you won't fall
Wealth truly is within, you just have to harness it
A solid bank account helps – study harder, hoe!
Being a dreamer can often bloom bitterness
Keep your mind right n anchor your rassclart
self!

I don't wish I could go back
but slyly *I wish* I could go back
to a time where laughter was free and nonsense
was all we knew . . .

*A portal forms, lights beaming and gliding from corner to corner
before finding the bearer of the wish. Filling their chest and finding
its way up the body. It controls them with Nike 'Just Do It' bags as the
keys to unlock their desires. Drawn to the bags like power-suited
amour, the bodies are pulled apart and stretched. Words fall from
their mouths without their permission:*

'Noooo word! ooof a lieee!
No. word. of. a. lieeee!
There was this one time!'

The portal leads them in dance and travel. They journey through hopscotch, skipping ropes, the Carlton and zigga zig ah. A kaleidoscope of colours, sounds, glitches and 90s–00s flavour going through time. Bleeding and blended futuristically:

Art Attack, ChuckleVision, Desmonds, Grange Hill, Queen's Nose, Alex Mack, The Bill, Rugrats, Arthur, Craig David, Cleopatra, So Solid, Damage, Sweet Female Attitude, Misteeq, Original Nuttah, Spice Girls, Sugababes, Britney, Brandy, TLC, Aaliyah, DMX, Tupac, Space Jam, Sabrina, Moesha, Sister Sister, etc.

LINK-UP

Being released from what feels like a migraine after a rollercoaster,
they arrive. Acknowledging their bodies' youthful metamorphosis,
and somewhat adult sentience. In part insult, part flattery (is dat u
yh?!) and all in love, they greet each other

Tolu	oiiiiii **this link-up is long overdue my Gs**

They clock the watchers.

Reena	yu man cooool yh?
Debz	hiii
Tolu	what's gUd!
Tia	wa gwarn! greetings n sal-U-Taytionz bruvaz / n sistas
Reena	rahh, ur cute still
Tia	dis girl
Reena	what yU saying?
Debz	*(weird audible nervous sound)*
Reena	am R 2-dah! double E 2-da / N 2 dah! –
Tia	her naaaaame is Shereene
Reena	Reena!
Debz	i'm Debz! she's Tia, she's –
Tolu	allow da government ting! Moodz init, dats baby D, Lady 7 and she's –
Reena	Lady Savage do u wanna hear me sing?
Debz	ooo sing for us
Tolu	sing if ur bad
Tia	ermm?? / right now?

Reena   what should i sing?

Debz   what about –

Reena   Wyen 2 bcum onnneee

> *Jumping in formation*
> *the girls become the*
> *South London Spices.*
> *Blackifying the chorus of '2 Become 1'*
> *(Spice Girls) in a way only they can.*

mi nii sum luv lyke mi nevah needed luv b4
Gonna be my peng ting baby (*etc.*)

Tolu   ok it's long now

Tia   alieee

Debz   yes Reena

Reena   Dash ur bb pin it's the only thing to doooo

Tia *drags* **Reena** *away*

Tia   apologies apologies!
sometimes my friends have no manners

Debz   who has / no manners?

Tolu   that's why / i'm not ur fren!

Reena   why u / cockblocking for?

Tia   do yu need some nourishment?

Tolu   let her be a sket / / if she wants to be

Tia   ooooo!!

Debz   behave! / when she starts now

Reena   You lot love preein' me!
Y dem ah watchiNN mii? / /
iz it pyurr je-loss-c'eeeee?
[MS DYNAMITE x SO SOLID]

Tia   blouse n skirt!

Tolu   jealousy? whooo

Reena   i don't wanna fight tonight uno

Debz   ooUU

Tolu   youuu don't want it /
                  u don't want MOODZ to get ferocious

Tia   don't wan it!

Reena   i'm a luvah not a fightah

Tolu   shook head

Debz   oU u gonna have dat?

Tia   don't have it!

Reena   i thought u had ur man

Tia/Debz who!?

Reena   didn't *yU* and SOMTO lock lips!?

Nollywood-inspired dramatic response

Tia/Debz violationnnnn

Tolu   how dare u! //
                  all that crust??

Tia   Somto you know

Debz   'low it

Hyped table banging/stomping

DING DING DING

> **Debz+Tia** *loosely take 'opposing' sides*
> *joining in with adlibs, lines and echos*
> *as they emcee battle*

Reena   yes! ur crusty lip man
yes! ur crusty lip *mannnn*!!
don't come for meeee!
don't come for meeee
i may be pretty but
i'm SAVAGE wid it
LETHAL wid it
full on – full on
Tekken the PISS
dis Nina WILL
slap u up!
scrap u up!
snap – crackle – pop u up!
dat n dat n BAD u UP!

Tolu   BAD UP who? what? where? how??
BAD UP who? what? where? how??
If u do mi right – ya got a friend 4 lyfe
if ya treat mi nice – yu'll only catch I side
otherwise – o dah wize!
i may be liable – 2 tek ya lyfe!
so hold it tight – give yu I life line!
give yu I life line! so HOLD it tight!!

Reena   I life line? I life line?
I life line is all i need
so tek time!
tek tek tek time!
coz it's SAVAGE play time
gal better kno
it's SAVAGE play time
am threatenin!
am deafenin!

gal better kno
i bring the reckonin
jammer u in
hammer u in
bar 4 bar
slew yu yu – him n her
slew yu yu – him n her

Tolu   slew who? what? where? how?
slew who? what? where? how?
time 4 savage 2 meet her ruin
amma jawbreaker!
no sweet tingz here
ur stars will burst N gum get bubbled!
u want moodz 2 get gloomy?
jest with me
u want moodz 2 get moody?
mess with me
u want moodz 2 get unruly?
ain't no mystery
u playin wid de darkside
best believe!!

Reena   ooo darkness
lick my lips – inhaling it
Batman 'n' am
shelling it
word to NoLay
i'm snatching bladders
snatching heifers
snatching wankers
cannibal wid it
glow up wid it
pull your heart out n am luvin it
eat ur guts n am spinach wid it
pop-pop-pop den **eyeee'm OUT**

Tolu   u need to back it
u need to back it

coz if i done her dance
she'll be all gone init
slaughtered, slain, sleepy hollow
ghost of ur ex boyfriends on my halo
supernatural! obliteration!
exterminate U like God did Sodom!
bring the fire
bring the flames
bring the flood
bring the Kane
u don't stand a chance – wid dis reign
chokeslam – big boot – against the ring
Dexter's Lab over Pinky's brainnnnn
i'm coming thru DU DU DU
feel the pain – verbal bullets
don't catch a stray
it's Terminator
u'll be my ashtray
a violator
a violator
ninja turtle
i'll shredDER U
wrath – I – yell
i'll Splinter U!
rebel U!!
lord of mic
i'm violator

They have to physically stop **Tolu**
as she violates to infinity

cheese and bread
a violator –
lord of mic
i'm violator
a violator –

Tia   it's enoughhhhh

Debz   jhezzzzz

Tia   my g

Reena   dat was hard still

Tolu   obviouslEE
               dat . . . dat was sick innit?

Ree/Debz/Tia
               obviouslEE!!!

PORTAL FLASH

WAY BACK WHEN

In Shakespearean form and hosting command with the groundedness of Denzel and all the grit south London brings. The following words are spoken:

Tia   Tamagotchis, Pokemon and alien babies.
             no word of a lie
             no word of a lie
             a time when you couldn't be on the phone
             and the internet at the same time.
             a time when floppy disks reigned!
             where flip phones or a brick were your right hand
             blades!
             happy slaps wasn't so happy and before whatsapp
             duppied msn!
             dose dayz? ahh, wayyyyyy back when!?
             responsibility freeeee!
             for the first time?
             a girl with brown skin and braids was a princess
             and Whitney was my fairy godmother
             we were living the life
             we juss didn't know it

Debz   do you remember!?

                                        Getting ready for school

                    'Cleopatra comin' atcha!'

HAIR   –   LIP GLOSS   –   BAG   –   HUBBA BUBBA

                    90s Choice FM jingle

                                        The bus stop

Tolu   some of the best and
             worst times of my school life
             was **on the bus**
             whether it was –

Debz   jumping off the open number 12!
              coz my Tamagotchi fell out

Reena   we could hop in and out!

Tia   routemaster ting!

Debz   before the bendies!

Tolu   or da timez when yutez from Ramzi
              thought they wanted to get rowdy

Reena   or da timez when Tia smashed da plate from
              technology on dat girl's head / / bad gyal!!

Tolu   mhad ting!!

Tia   orrrrrrr the timez wen we
              woz just . . . uno, enjoying each
              othas companyyy???

Debz   hate it when u get vex

Tia   it was self defence

Reena   from her mouth?

Tia   Malcolm X said / 'by any means' –

Reena/Tolu/Debz
              come on!/ughhh/not now!

Tolu   theeese were the times
              when my dad was scamming me

Reena   419 and dat

Debz   original hustler!

Tolu   talking bout *'if your brotha*
              walks you half way it builds resilience?'
              making my older bruva drop me to the bus stop???
              how do i learn to protect myself with a chaperone
              you tell me? hmm? these times manz movin like a
              CIA spy ting! sent by top forces to stunt my
              growth

Tia	'CIA'?
Debz	top forces?
Reena	beggin it
Tolu	talking about safety in numbers blah blah / blahhhh –
Debz	well at least you have a dad who cares annddddd who can actually spend time with you
Tolu	ah ahh

*Tolu gets **Debz** into a headlock*

Reena	ahh ahhh
Tia	ahhh ahhhh
Debz	stoppp!
Reena	why do you need a dad? when you have me!

Debz** gets out, chases **Tolu

Tia	when you have WE!
Debz	annoying!
Tolu	greed is not good uno

Reena** is annoying **Tia

Reena	yh Deb-bor-rah
Tia	move Reena man!
Debz	u should be happy to have brothers
Tolu	'low it
Debz	at least you know how to grips some1 up!
Tia	EVV-REE-DAY!

***Tia** karate chops on each syllable*

They play fight, imitating brothers

Reena	that's what happens when you have to defend yourself in a house full ah boys
Tia	it was mad dem times!
Tolu	and my oldest Julius always made it madder he was the one causing the trouble
Reena	always ready to jump on anyone **at any timeeee!!**
Tolu	if it wasn't for him i woulda had ma independence 4rm long time! n boys wouldn't have avoided me for THREE whole yearzz
Tia	that wasn't the reason

Tolu *claps the back of* **Tia***'s head*

Debz	he was so scary
Reena	what was the reason?
Tolu	can i finish?!

*they respond through
'mmm's and eye rolls*

thankfully, when i hit yr10
all that was over!
i buss case
i did my chores and became – **respeckt-ted**
i got the grades and became – **respons-ha-bull**
and most importantly
big bro went to uni
outside of London

*with claps and stomps
naturally they riff into praise and worship*

We are saying t'ank you Jesus
t'ank you my Lord
We are saying t'ank you Jesus
t'ank you my Lord

Tolu	this new found freedom
	came at the right time
	puberty hit
	which means i became a *woman*
	just before the last summer
	before all summers

Debz   wait, you got urs in class!?

Tia   goat! that was me

Debz   oh yhhhh

Tolu   dat day was a madness

Reena   not for you!!

PORTAL FLASH

Tia	my mum said it would happen soon
	so as usual i stay ready so i didn't
	have to **be ready**
	ur girl stayed strapped for months
	but the day when it finally came?
	ughhhhhh!!

School bell

Ms Georgeeee just wouldn't
let me out to get a pad

Tia *waves frantically*

Ms George
ERRR
Put your hand down, Tia!!

Tia
But Misssss
It's not fairR! you let Georgia go!

Ms George
Hand down now!!

Tia
I swear, I'm gonna have blood on my leg
This is against my rights as a woman!

Ms George
That's enough now

Tia
But Misssss

Reena *is secretly trying to
organise a distraction*

Ms George
If I turn around and your hand is still up?!

Reena
ahh Miss you're being badmind

Ms George
ERR!

Reena *signals* **Tia** *to exit*

Reena
Innit? Badmind!! Badmind!!

Students join in her raucous 'badmind'
Reena *throws a snapper and stink bomb*

snap *snap*
FUN SNAP BANG!

Students Making Up Noise
horrid! eww! that smell? Miss!?

Debz   operation **stink bomb**!

Reena   i got detention for a whole week

Reena *glares at* **Tolu**

Tolu   whatttt?
you know i woz NOT about to join dat operation,

	making up noise!? wen i was finally free? nah man!
Tia	that's why i love dese tew // more than u
Reena	yh yh yh
Debz	of / course
Tolu	lies! i'll always be the batman to ur robin //
Tia	wasteeeman
Debz	that doesn't make sense
Tolu	you know yu luurve me
Tia	movee
Reena	hello!! I had to use three pens to get thru all dose lines // *'i will – reflect – on my – behaviour'*
Tia	the real MVP! mi real freennn
Tolu	whateveeeerrrr! it wasn't bad for you U were prepped and not leaking everywhere! at least ur mum told you!
Tia	of course that's my bestie didn't ur marge tell you?

Poop?

Tolu	pooooop! i fought my period was poop
Tia	how?
Debz	pah-din?
Reena	nasty
Tolu	when i wiped it was brown // and –
Debz	what was?
Tia	are / you alright?

Reena	chattin shit – / literally!
Tolu	the tissue paper!? DUH!
Tia	it's us that she's 'duh'ing?
Tolu	kept washing my bum –
Debz	T M I
Tolu	but the brown kept coming back!
Tia	walking round wid poop inna ya crack? / lawd!
Tolu	it was blood you egg!
Tia	you didn't ask ur mum?
Tolu	i dunno i was / just –
Debz	scared? / that's ok
Reena	awww
Tolu	move! . . . she saw tissue in the bin and asked me about it
Debz	*'I was getting so worried, it's about time'*
Tolu	about time? she didn't even tell me
Tia	u know African parents don't talk man
Debz	paarring it
Reena	herrrrrrrr African parents
Tia	tell the truth and shame de devil //
Tolu	woow
Debz (*coughs*)	well –
Tia	it's true doe
Reena	don't clump them 2geda, coz mine –

Tia   ur half anyway / / dats why –

Debz   rude

Tolu   peak!

Tia   nah be honest!
               did *ur mum* talk to u bout sex?

Tolu   *'DON'T DO IT'*

Tia   there's this boy / 'n' –

Reena   *'FACE YOUR BOOK'*

Debz   *'BOYFRIEND KO? BOYFRIEND NI?'*

Tia   *'OPEN YA BOOK NOT YAH LEGS'*

Tolu   'SO YOU'VE GROWN WINGS'

Debz   *'TINK SEH YUH BAD?'*

Reena   *'WHEN I WOZ YOR H'AGE!!!'*

> *'Educational' statements from
> African and Caribbean parents
> fill the space*

'SEKKLE YOURSELF'
    'IF U LIKE BEAT ME'

' Yah tu fass'
                'Instead of . . .'
         'Tink say ur big woman'
'PUT IT ON MY HEAD'
                'Little girl! Little girl!'
'YU CANNOT COME AND KILL ME'
         'You will end up in McDonald's'

> *Richard Blackwood's
> 'Mama Used to Say'
> dominates the space*

ON THE BUS

Tolu   sooooo, after i realised it wasn't poop
              dat wouldn't go away *even after*
              i showered pubescence wasn't so bad

Tia   pubescence!? //

Reena   datz ur fren

Debz   our friend

Tolu   I FINALLY! had responsibilities!
              an freedom to get ish done
              and ma first mission?

B B Q

Tolu   back of the bus **Queens**
              just like Aaliyah
              we coming thru

Reena   hot – like – fiyah
              [AALIYAH]

Debz   R – vibes – will

              take you **higher**
              and higher
              and higher
              and higher

Tia   princesses would've been more accurate
              but de P wasn't poppin like the **Q!**

Debz   when ur sitting up dere
              right at da back
              itz like da throne
              itz like mufasa looking over the proudlands

Reena   pride lands

Debz   u can see everything and everyone

Tolu   sniper views
best situation to stay ready
so u don't have to **be ready**
(*Shade.*) PLUS *if u wasn't allowed out after school*

Reena   or ur connexion's spot was **lock off**

Tolu   u could always rely on TFL for nuff jokes
it was a sustainable plan

Tia   and it didn't matter which bus

Debz   long az it was in **souf**

Tolu   WHEN I SAY SOUTH YOU SAY RUN TINGZ
SOUTH
RUN TINGZ
SOUTH
RUN TINGZ
BRAAAAAPP!

Reena   wooly road to be precise

In extra RP
David Attenborough

Tia   12 – 171 – 148 – 68 – 176 –
Sometimes 63 on an old kent ting
like a web
4rm all our bitz
4rm garage to Elephant

Tolu   as long as WE got on it?!
respect had to be shown

Reena   dats right coz all of the
mandem respected me //

Debz   yes Reena!

Tia   why must u –

Reena   give love?

ehhhh

Reena	because mi love giving! // woii
Tolu	man lyke!
Debz	Jesuz!
Tia	dutty gyal!
Reena	reeyy! //
Tia	woiii
Tolu	i will never forget the jokes!
Reena	the bruddahs
Tia	the pervs
Debz	the **beeeeef**
Tolu	and sometimes truces! between us and the other schools on endz

PORTAL FLASH

this one time
on the way to our places of edu-mah-cation
the bus was a battlefield

    we jumped into formation with the weight
    of a thousand kenyans
    clocked our surroundings quick time
    drawed out da tools

flour   **water**

    egg

Tolu	a full on war broke out

ARE YOU READY TOOO
suckkkkk ittttttttt
[WWE DX CHANT]

90s cult action film finale
music fades in

oiiiiiii   duckkk!   mine-out!!   peeeeakk dickhedddd!

move!!   r U dumbbb   watch out!!   paaaarr

The BBQs are dishevelled

Tolu   course . . . da B-B-Q . . . shut it . . . down

yaaa . . . DUN . . . know

we were doing up breakfast brawl
on the top deck of the 171
no malice
just jokes!
nuff madness
and IOUs

Tia   apart from the commuters

Old Annnnieee

Debz   'where's my Sun!'

Reena   tomorrow tomorrow!! [ANNIE MUSICAL]

Tia   always in one corner of Heygate

Debz   singing or harassing you for coins

Tia   the police had love for her thou

Reena   obviously she's why'ite!

Tia   but be it one of us!

Tia/Reena/Tolu
righttt!

Debz   no chance! you can't be black
AN' have mental problems uno!

Tia   u haffi pick one!

Tolu   yu remember when Adam n dem
would pay her to sing?

ohhh yhhhh

Debz   they were boyin' it

Reena	but she loved it
Debz	she was finished
Tia	she was lucky! sometimes being finished is how you survive the dunyaaa
	trueeeee sayyyy
Tolu	better to laugh dan cry
	mmm! (*In joyful pentecostal prophetic confirmation.*)
Tia	i cannot come and **dieeeee!**
Reena	better to be BLIND than SEE ur haters
Tolu	u / wot?
Debz	Reena?
Tia	no lyke, no!?
Tolu	anywayyyy **leg itttt!** dashed off the bus! driver called Scotland Yard rolled up super LATE pancake mix all over our uniforms! got detention my privileges? revoked! Dad dropped me to school for like three months but that was deffo one of the best mornings **ever**!!!
Tia	and before u judge us
Tolu	judge whoo!?
Reena	if ya wan judge suck ya muddah!!
Tolu	everybody shits
Debz	everybody farts

Tia	what they mean is . . . we weren't ur typical teenagers / things –
Reena	yes we was
Tia	it was not all roses though!
Tolu	what is?
Tia	typical teenagers have parents who can afford to spend time with dem
Debz	maybe we should –
Tia	typical teenagers don't mourn boyfriends at fourteen?
Tolu	Tia!?
Tia	typical teenagers don't share one room / with three other –
Reena	why u tellin dem for!?
Tia	what i'm trying to say is . . . this this nonsense? was our release when tings got sour whenever it got tu much whenever we . . . we couldn't stop time . . .
Debz	think happy thoughts!!
Tolu	happy thoughts **onlyyyyy**

All BBQ join in,
Reena *gives Xtina vocals*

Tia	ur doing too much
Reena	ur doing too little

PORTAL FLASH

YEAR 11

NO ~~PARENTAL GUIDANCE~~

Reena	when we wasn't stressing about exams we stayed grateful coz we could finally touch Trocadero **with no parental guidance**
Debz	and the glass museum!?
Reena	The Millennium Dome??!!!???
Debz	everyone wanted to go
Tolu	dat was way off endz i didn't wanna go
Tia	of course not
Reena	you need 2 be more adventures uno
Tia	true say
Tolu	Narm got a new library
Reena	dis girl
Debz	**these were** da times where we'd **cotch** under the pink elephant by the castle up the slope and under the white canopy
Reena	Choppin on chupa chups!
Tolu	looking out for my man with the dvds
Tia	setting our sights higher!
Tolu	dis was the spot for the grown lot
Reena	15 going on 16
Debz	16 going on 17
Reena/Tia	
	and college bruddahs

Reena/Tia/Tolu *growl in delight*

Debz   don't know what it was about
             that final year but these lot became boy crazy

Reena   mmm

Tolu   ooo weeee

Reena   looking slender and fineee
             MMM mine!

Tia   we had no business being there
             but all our bizness – was there!

Debz   watching all the buses drive by
             London in the summertime!?
             felt like sky was the limit
             as we took in the metropolis view
             the blue clouds, all the skyscrapers . . .

Reena   as we took in the buff tingz

Tolu   peng tinz

Tia   leng tingz

Debz   as we took in everything our world was made of –

Reena   uno the Fundamental boyz, Bow Wows //
             J-Boogs, the Omarions

Debz   hey!!

Tia   the Craig Davids, Ushers // Will Smiths

Debz   hello!!!

Tolu   the Harveys, the Wileysss, // the –

Reena/Tia
             whoooo?

Debz   i'm trying to help dem visualise here!

Tolu   ok ok! we spent many weekends
             strolling around Elephant

Reena   looking for man!

Tolu/Tia uuhhhh?

Debz no // nooo

Tolu see your friend!

Tia Reena!

Debz put her somewhere please!

Reena i'm just playing man

> *They journey through like an obstacle course*

Debz we was in, out and around the centre!

Reena hit the stalls for the latest CDs!
bamboos! Shambalas!

Tia touch tescos!

Tolu and of course anytime we saw one?
we'd **hit Greggs!**

Reena didn't have to sneak into bowling
coz we were finally out of dem nun uniforms
yuck! these were da times where
we'd pass the Portuguese cafes
shout *hey **papiiii*** den
'leg it!'
swing back-round

Tia tunnel through the station

Debz corner through New Kent

Reena and reach **Wooly Road**

Tolu long for no reason alie?

Tia when we cudda walked straight
but we rarely did

Reena first we'd hit the library!
the museum upstairs
was low key the spot for the elitist dates

dem times derr

Debz   playing with the artifacts / made me
feel so intellectual –

Reena   objects?

Tolu   and McDonald's across the road
was a chef's kiss bonus

Tia   unless being a penny sweet seller
levelled you up
so you could afford Nando's
on da roundabout!
dem times derr ya nah!

Debz   my mum worked with the
council across the road
so there was noo way
i was linking anyone

Reena   yh she would lick you down

Debz   oh, like how ur mum licked the
McFlurry out ur hand? –

Tolu/Tia   uH!

Debz   and dragged u by ur collar into the car?

Tolu/Tia   uH!

Tolu   think ur a badman inni

They hype up **Debz**

HEARTLESS

but you'd still step through the Arch of East Street
for dem Nike knockoffs
3210 cases – top up your **five – day – pass**
and den hit Greggs

Nokia 3210 ringtone

dem times deehrrrr!

if it wasn't Greggs it was Bagel King

Tia	if it wasn't Bagel King it was jerk chicken
Reena	if wasn't jerk chicken it was Safeways and if it wasn't Safeways?
Debz	it was MK Oneeee?! coz we had no money *strictly* eye shopping

but come summertime??

Reena	we'd branch even further hit all of our bitz
Tia	apart from mine!!
Tolu	who's trekking to Blue Borough, cuz?
Tia	Catford is not that far! it's right after Narm
Reena	u lieeee!
Debz	it iz kinda far, Tia
Tia	in yr10 we moved out of ends and now dese lot act like they got amnesia
Debz	it's ok, h'itz . . . we can't all be from the righteous side of souf
Tia	gweh gweh!

Tia *chases them*

Reena	we'd cut through East Street
Debz	breeze through *Aylesbury*
Tia/Tolu	*Aylesbury!!*
Reena	my bitz! n it was always –
Debz	interesting

Tolu/Tia   shookhead/really?!

Reena   ur top lip is interesting!

Debz   so is your forehead

Tolu   eh?!

Reena   ur getting brave ya na

Tia   as she should be

Tolu   my G

Debz   u said i needed to be slicker with comebacks

Reena   not with me!

Tolu (*proud*)
        u've created a monster

Tia   tu tu'z yh, black girls soon to be black queens /
        we don't call ourselves such

Tolu   is it everyday Rosa Parks?

Reena   anyway after cotching round my bit,
        we'd come out by Albany
        and through to **the sea of green**

                                    PORTAL FLASH

        Burgess Park

Debz   do you remember Fun Day with Som-toeee?

                                    Somto appears

and **the pigeon**

                                    The pigeon appears

ahhhhh

Tolu   dat stick he always carried!!

Debz   dat Kobe jersey he wouldn't take off!

Reena   dat likkle cream. crust. ting! *around his mouth*

Debz   this crust has really offended you //

Reena   crusty!

Tolu   nahhh do you remember Somto's
               battered hand-me-down size 10 Kickers /
               dat were always **always** talking!

Tia   violating!

SOM-TOE AHH-DOE-MAH-KO

Debz   dare my man to do anything
               anytinnnnnnnnnnnnnn
               and he's on it!!

Tolu   a pioneering spirit of a sombody!

Debz   Deanne goes

Deanne
'Ayyoo Somto i bet you can't catch that pigeon'

Debz   then he goes

Somto
'. . . Hold my Rubicon'

Random Announcer
Live and direct from Burgess is Crruustyy Somto Vs Crust-ty Pi-geon

Debz   it's a showdown folks!
                  he ran so fastttt yhhh–

Tia   like Superman catching a ride from Sonic –
               on TOP OF the lightning ears of FLASH himself
               kinda fast?
               or like an African uncle eyeing the last plate of
               jollof kinda fast?

Reena   neek of da world

Debz   man bolted innit!
               he dashes across the park
               with the speed of a hundred JA-MAY-CANS

his hands shoot out of his sockets
like Seaman saving a ball
like Jordan dunking in Space Jam
like a black mother clapping vaseline into the face
of her child
he caught it / with one –

Tia   rahtid did he really catch it?

Tolu   don't you remember?

Reena   why would she?
             dis gyal was by the tyres with Niel

Tolu   k – i – / s – s – i – n – g!

Tia   don't jealous / me

Reena   have you seen me? / meee!

Tia   ahhh / ahhh –

Debz   errm
             hello
             hi
             shut it!!!!!

             he – caught – it!!!
             swooped up the pigeon with
one
             swift
grab!

> *They look at their hands in disgust*
> *before fleeing in chaos*

eww   bird flu   mad   nah   'low it   bush boy!

Random Announcer
By God he's done it.
London's most ferocious and disrespectful species
has been caught!

> *They're disarranged*

Tolu   now dis fool!

Reena   dis doughhh-nut.

Tia   dis bruddah!

Debz   dis egg
                is chasing us lot!
                with this detty bird in his hands!
                he's creasing

Tolu   i'm crying!

Debz   i SWEAR DA ting has brushed
                my **top lip** and **it's CHAOS**
                all i can hear is Deanne in the background like

Deanne
*'Somto caught AH pigeon! NOW . . . you see,
dat bird – can't fly!!??'*

Cosigns x hype

Debz   and the mandem
                doin' up call and response
                like *pigeon, pigeon*

Nuff Yutes
ehhhh pigeon, pigeon
Somto caught ah pigeon now you see dat bird can't fly
Somto caught ah pigeon now you see dat bird can't fly
pigeon, pigeon ah pigeon, pigeon

Debz   no one went near Somto
                for like **two weeks** after coz –

Reena   man was spreading bird flu!!

Debz   the foolish thing?
                is that i believed it!
                do you remember the
                unprovoked **stoopidnessssss** we did?
                no behaviourrrr

Tolu   no home training

Tia   but we had home training!

Debz   we'd leave the butterfly arch
                cross to the BP

Reena   Past Bethwin!

Tia   and hit Iceland for dem 8pack Screwballs
                TWO POUNDS
                and Capri-Sun packs
                ONE POUND
                which would be the perfects sides
                4 wings – chips – drink
                ONE POUND FIFTY
                Tennessee chicken
                these were my bitz – *before we moved*
                cut thru the estates!

Tolu   adventure playground

Reena   Blue Elephant

Debz   tower blocks

Tia   come out on Medler
                maybe get our nails done
                or diamontes fixed
                pass the bingo
                cross the road
                stunt around **Slick Ricks**

Tolu   the peoples spot

Debz   i never went inside

Tia   a community hub (*reassures*)

Reena   the barbers?!?

Tia   before heading to

                                    PORTAL FLASH

Camberwell Green park

They look at **Reena**

Debz   ahhh

Reena   just finished piercing her ears
              whennn / she left me for dead

Debz   i didn't have Claire's money

Reena   it was hot – everyone was about
              but it was also hot as in lava
              the air was thick with
              B-O, Lynx, Dax and Blue Jeans
              it was HOT fam
              i was minding my business
              trying to stay cool
              being a gud citizen . . . doodling
                 uno graffin da bench
              true say i got A* in art so was blessing the endz
              with one of my many talents
              whilst these hooligans?
              were war-ring with water bombs
              so how did i?? how did iiiiii???
              become the target plz?

Dog growls and barks

Debz   blood of GEEZOS!

                    CASTLE!!!!

Tia   our saving grace
              the climbing ting with a slope
              and a rope on da back end

Tolu   you'd tink Tarzan trained us
              wid da way we climbed dat wooden ting
              then we clocked!??

Tolu/Debz/Tia
              Reeeenaaaaa!!!

Tolu   that's when dis dog basically / came 'n' –

Reena   dog?? dog?!?
              dogs are friendly
              jaws foaming
              dat.
              fat.
              burnt.
              caramel.
              child eating. chuckie look alike pit!
              ran towards me like i was premium ox tail!

              our father who art in heaven
              please get me out of this and
              i promise to stop sneaking back in after 9 p.m.
              to join the youth choir this sunday
              and stop blaming my sister
              for the missing forks!

                                                    Dog barks

              each side of the castle was filled
              i thought i was done!
              NYAM
              FINISHED
              then i saw the rope
              swinging towards me
              these lot finally decided to help
              channelled everything i had
              ugh – trying to pull – ughhhhh
              myself up dat ting!!!
              it turns out my inner Lara Croft has no stamina
              two grips and i fell

Tia   pit bull chuckie had no mercy
              didn't blink once

Tolu   chased her up and down!

Reena   with its tongue at my heels
              shoe fell off

internal prayers
legs sprinting
external screaming
taunts from the castle
the beast gleaming
two laps across and around
before one '**UNCLE!**'
    with an umbrella rescued me
he whacked the ground
tried to distract it but
that MUTT kept coming
      bang!
missed again
      bang!
missed again!
    Uncle please please!
GBOSA!!

                      Dog whines

this gremlin barely flinched???

Owners
HE'S ONLY PLAYING!

all of a sudden the owners showed up

Owners
DOG'S ONLY PLAYING, MATE!

Random Uncle
DOES SHE LOOK LIKE SHE'S PLAYING!?

Reena   uncle saviour left
handed me back my shoe
finally able to catch my breath
i turned around . . .
stacked busses back to back to back
fully packkkkkked
traffic on a hot summer's day
and i was the entertainment – **what an L**

never changed my weave so fast
nuff ppl on endz kept asking
'was dat u?' 'it was u init'
for two weeks straight – **what an L**

> **Tolu** *begins to clap*
> **Tia** *and* **Debz** *recognise the rhythm*
> *The clapping beat evolves as they join in*
> *adlibs of 'you a survivor' and*

> *'go, Reena'*
> *'you're alive'*
> *'you didn't die'*
> *'you survived'*

Reena *dances.*

PORTAL FLASH

HIT UP NARM

Tolu   days when we cud reach all our bits
           were not easy to come by / so –

Debz   so we cherished them dearly!

Reena   moist //

Tolu   strolled –

Tia   strolled around till blue turned deep purple

Debz   turquoise first

Reena   these b-tech Matildas

Tia   dats why you flopped english //

Tolu/Debz
           AH

Reena   i got a B

Tia   B 4real //

Tolu   BUT! –

Debz   but when we got tired –

Tolu   WE'D! buck one of my olders!!

Reena   links.

Tolu   thennnn we'd
           hit up Narm
           in a whip
           feeling bahd!
           glideee past Frontline

Debz   **cruise** through Yellow Brick
           which *sometimes was a **mixed blessing***

Tolu   it was home

Tia/Debz/Reena   to you!!

Tolu   to we
             to i
             to u 2-nite
             it's Rye-Lane time //
             let's feast not fight

Reena   dead

Tia   we're in (*show location*)

Debz   man were disappearing
             through walls in ur estate
             and ur proud?

Tia   BOMB-BA!

Reena   watch ah!

Tolu   i don't entertain / gossippp!
             dis nollywood talk?

Reena   don't have ittttt

Debz   back me please? back it! /
             was dis not a ting?

Tolu   chattin shittttt

Debz   Tolu don't lie! Reena!? Tia?!

Reena   facing my front

Tia   umhm! dis iz Africa's fight //

Tolu   dumb!

Debz   coz whenever i bucked ma cuzins
             who went W.P. they had
             nuff stories about juju //
             roadman and juju

Tia   obeah!

Reena	say swear?!
Debz	for uno, protectionsssss
Tolu	gossipers!
Reena	linking wizards yh
Tolu	whateverrrr
Debz	we still love u
Tolu	all you know is gossip ur supposed to be on my side Debz
Tia	which side!? / whhichhhh
Reena	yh which side?! / hmmm?
Tolu	jollof!
Tia	rice n peas!

> **Tia**, **Reena** *and* **Tolu** *go*
> *into 'fake beef' on sight mode*

Debz these were the good times
doing everything and nothing
and always alwaysssss **vibing**

> *an old skool grime beat disrupts the space,*
> *they lean into their favourite flows*

Yu-da-ga Nod-da-got Ba-da-gad
Yu-da-ga Nod-da-got Ba-da-gad

Debz + Tolu
i'll pop your bubble bubble
step up to me and you'll be in trouble trouble
step to me and I'll burst your bubble bubble
[D DOUBLE E]

Neek 1 neek 2
Neek 1 neek 2
[SO SOLID TWIN]

all your friends are clapped too
[LETHAL B]

tooooo clapped!!!

Tia + Reena
so fresh and clean
so fresh and clean
In-nigh-ya-late man like listerine
mans not Casper but i'll ghost your bars **bars**

You're washed
You're dead

Debz + Tolu
You're tapped
You're dread

Tia + Reena
I'm not friendly
I'm so crude
I'm rude

Reena
Imma mood

Tolu
Half past 6 to the half past 4
Step on the stage like war
Never never – ever TRY be clever

Be spittin more lyrics than even ever

Debz
And my mind so clean
And my creps so fresh

Imma black skin queen never test

Tia
never pressed
never stressed

Tolu
I'm a God
Don't NEED to BE
better than the rest

Reena
In-see-cu-rities
give it a back slap
Don't chat to me
on black chat
[STOOSHIE]

Tia
I'm strong –

Debz
I'm firm

Reena
Don't need a man to confirm

Don't let the man dem
open sesame
Fix up your mind
love you incessantly
Man dem
get on your grind
that is the key
Don't you know
that you're
kings internally!!
[MIGRAINE SKANK]

BRraaaaaaarrrrttttttt!!!
Brapppppp!!!

Others calm **Tolu** *down*
as she over-hypes

ADAM + JESUS

Adam and Jesus
'THAT WAS HARD STILL'

Tia   that's how we met
             Adam and Jesus

Debz   blasphemy!

Reena/Tolu
             double trouble

Tia   one was team Mario, darkskinnn
             so we called him Adam
             uno the original man!

Deb   mr say ur just a friend

Tolu   hyped! cracking jokes always

Deb   loud. extremely loud.
             stamping his territory
             eating all the food

Reena   he was sick at art like me
             his Lil Kim in the desert drawing!??
             phenomenal! / amazing!

Tia   super intelligent as well
             his mind was everywhere
             knew all this stuff about computers –
                 helped me transform my MySpace page
             and about African ppl before *colonialists* came!
                 uno, tings they didn't teach us in school

Debz   but den he would say something random
             like how female spiders nyam
             males spiders after getting their babies
             yuck!

Tolu   and the other one, team Chris Brown

Tia	caramel!
Tolu	but with long braids always **singing!**
Reena	yoooo/oooo [CHRIS BROWN]
Tolu	the new type he was . . . different
Debz	born in America
Reena	shades. velour tracksuit air force ones fashion boy walked around like he was badder dan Naomi and his trainer collection was **MAHD!** couldn't tell him nuffin rocked half blonde, half black braided pigtails and still bagged all the girls!?
Tolu	but would rock ur jaw if u wanted to get brave!
Debz	and he always gave the best fashion advice! said he liked my creps
Tolu	taught me bout dat 5 finger discount
Reena	and it was hard to catch one without the other and all the girls wanted demmm
Debz	i didn't
Reena/Tolu/Tia	mmmm
Tolu	but our group ting was different it was like the missing puzzle 'peace-ez' like Niecey and Kim

Debz   like Justin and Britney

Tolu   like Kenan and Kel

Debz   uno like we knew each other
in a past life . . . / or something
it. just. fits

Tolu   this girl

Tia   let it go babes

Reena   and they were rudeeeee
a1 insults that wud send yu
back 2 ur mums womb in doom!

Tia   anyone could get it!

Debz   ur mum's so slow, it takes her 3 years to count 3
pence!

Tolu   ur dad's sooo ugly, his face makes people vomit
on sight

Tia   ur sister is so stupid / she –

Reena   dutty stinking she **BEEP** whore shuddah drown!

Debz/Tolu/Tia
Reena!

Reena   what!? you guys are given dem the PG version!!
let me provide the –

PORTAL FLASH

Tia   omdzzz it was themmmm who invited us to
HAMMED'S DRINK-UP

THE TALENT SHOW

Cassette tape plugged in **Debz** *is dancing her heart out to y2k rock music in her room:*

'Teenage Dirtbag' (Wheatus)
<fwfwfwfwfw>
'Don't Let Me Get Me' (P!nk)
<fwfwfwfwww>
'Bring Me to Life' (Evanescence)

The girlz barge in

Reena	i'm not going unless u man take this seriously or we can practise 2mrw
Tolu/Tia	no!
Reena	this why u can't answer ur phone? //
Tolu	we've only lost fyve minutes
Debz	i'm sorry i was lost in the –
Reena	ughhhh //
Tia	calm down
Tolu	she's gonna explode
Debz	where do u wanna start?
Reena	from the top! go through it once so i can see u've ALL been practising
Tia	such a bossy boots / she's so bossy man
Tolu	why can't we dooo what we always doo?
Tia	yh we already kno the verses
Debz	'n' i can't get to ur britney levels
Reena	ok bye then go

Tolu/Tia   ughhh / ahh

Debz   it's my house though

Reena   routine or bun u lot

Debz   Adam said we shouldn't be
late for Hammed's drink-up

Tolu   he won't show up till late anyway

Reena   we do the routine
n den u can think of a rap
for the introduction
deal or no deal?

. . .

Tolu/Debz/Tia   deal

Reena   exactly!

> *Opening with a harmony of*
> *'Tearin Up My Heart' (N Sync)*
> *They dance in the truest form of*
> *'American pop' and 'RnB white boy band'*

BACKSTREET BOYS: LARGER THAN LIFE/EVERYBODY
N SYNC: BYE BYE BYE/GONNA BE ME MASHUP
BRITNEY/XTINA: CRAZY/'GENIE'/SLAVE 4 U, etc.
Record scratch

Debz   OK . . . I LIED
it was a littleee
more like this

Reena   Moodz grab the sticks! /
get into place!

Tia   chill out terminator

Debz   is this a new formation?

Reena   move

Tolu   don't snatch it from my hands like dat!

There's chaos, calamity, and swag throughout
their 'music video'-esque choreography.
Reena *channels pop rnb icons, conducting*
whilst dancing, snapping the squad into shape.
Tolu *is the star in her own foxy world,*
Debz *is lost, Tia is fixated on the counts*

JAMELIA: MONEY
PINK: MOST GIRLS
MYA: CASE OF THE EX, etc.
Record scratch

Reena	SIS SIS SIS! this arch?? have you not been listening to Vybz?
Debz	i have
Tia	it's not translating
Debz	teach me then! look . . . . . . it doesn't . . . . . .
Tolu	almost . . .
Tia	u haffi bend like Beckham curve!
Tolu/Reena	
	and bend!
Debz	i can't whine like u guys
Reena	ok so, just . . . just . . . it's ur nyash not ur back

They demonstrate their advice

Debz	can i just sing something? neverrrrrrrrrrrrrrrrrrrr wudda made it [MARVIN SAPP]

Tia   and i can read something from / maya ang –

Reena   nobody wants to hear
                ur b2k fan-fiction

Tolu/Debz
                oo i do

Tia   they're epic romances and scripts

Reena   wannabe writers via bebo, no thanks!

Tia   we can do more dan dance n sing though
                drop some rhythm and poetry? click for me!!

                                        Tolu and **Debz** click

   Tia recites an iconic line from a black 90s sitcom with a poetic flow

Tolu   ok / t-boogie!

Reena   that was dry

Debz   we're like Lauryn Hill!

Reena   i give up!

Tia   ur doing too much

Tolu   she's tew facety man

Debz   init tell her

                                    Reena notices **Debz** wall
                                            as she walks away.

Reena   errmmm where's TLC? Mis-Teeq?

Tolu   or Dynamite?

Tia   what kind of white shrine is this?

Debz   don't act like you don't like Britney

Tia   yhhh her muuuuussssssssic /
                her music!! but i'm not tryna look like her

Debz   i didn't say –

Tolu   chill

Tia	laaaaaaawwwwwwwwwd! why is there no black woman on this wall?
Debz	Spice Girls is right there
Tolu	Spice Girls
Debz	Melanie C, Mel B!?
Tia	what are these circles?

They react to circles

Reena	u tryna get plastic surgery?
Tolu	leave her man! with what money?
Tia	this isn't funny
Tolu	this isn't NipTuck
Reena	u don't need that
Tia	what the heck man the darker the berry?[1] . . .
Reena	if we're not / rehearsing yh –
Tia	the darker the berry!!!
Debz	the sweeter the juice . . .
Tia	pardon?!
Debz	THE DARKER THE BERRY!!! THE SWEETER / THE JUICE . . . THE DARKER the fleSH-uh! the deeper the . . . (*trails off*)
Tia	louder!

Tia *removes the posters*

i'll knock you out u know

---

1 Line referencing Pam Grier in *Foxy Brown* (film, 1974).

Reena   Tia!

Tolu   relax mannn

Tia   first person to throw God into things
but must have forgotten that He made u?
look at ur skin!? look at ur skin Debz
ur buff! how many times do i have to tell u?

Debz   stop gassing me, man

Tia   tell her pls

Tolu   are u dizzy? look at ur face

Reena   are u dumb? buff ting!

Tia   skin rich like sugar!

Tolu   lookin like a chocolate strawberry

Reena   skin smooth like a babies bottom

Tia   melanin strong like a Ugandan queen

Tolu   lips sparkling like a crown

Reena   forehead bright as gold

Tia   body set gooood! and ur mind too.
for real though, if u put these up!?
with circles, again!

Debz   i won't . . . i wont . . .thank you
group huggggg

Tia/Tolu/Reena
eww/moist/'low it

Debz   NOW!!!

> **Debz** *pulls everyone*
> *into a group hug*
> *The girls get 'glammed up'*
> **Debz** *is lost in thought*

Debz   i used to have this crazy complex, used to . . .
my mum remarried and now 'my family'
doesn't look like me, quick to speak on
what i'd eat, how i spoke . . .
quick to remind me how
'you must've taken after your dad'
blah blah blah, they policed me for a hot min
genetics is butters
coz me and my mum looked nothing alike
people would ask if she was my babysitter!?
didn't bust me her long hair, clear skin, flat
stomach or . . .
but then Tia started policing me which
i promise u is worse!
she might growl if you try to hug her
or say *shut up* if you tell her u luv her
but really n truly, she's a typical
softy wiv ah hard shell
Tia smelled like summer, uno explorative
dragging us to Southbank?! like we were tourists
coz she *always* wanted to stay out! and WALK! or
READ! she never forgot a book that's for sure!
she use to lose stuff all time
house keys, gel, bus pass – super forgetful!
finding her stuff in ur house was the norm
just littering herself in places like she was tryna
leave a trail . . .
maybe it's coz she always wanted to be out?
hmphs . . . that night she left me a note
saw it a few days later in my coat pocket
her leaving *stuff* where you didn't *expect*
meant you'd have *stuff* showing up
just when you needed it

Tolu   yo!

Reena   can we go now?

Debz   yeah one sec

Tia   Debz you had all this time to change

Reena   wear dat tight top n hurry up

Tolu   you know she wants to
              look good for Adam

Reena   fam! she'll catch up!

HAMMED'S DRINK-UP

A super micro mix of 90s garage/grime

DJ
H'INSIDEE H'INSIDEE
UKNOW WHAT TIME IT IZ

BLUE LIGHTS – PAPER PLATES – **DAGGERING**

The drink-up erupts in
teenage dancehall daggering madness
Reena *is the life of the party, enjoying catching and giving whines*
when she gets spun around

MWAH
Lights blast on as the DJ scratches

Reena	u lipsed me?! oh my God! oh my God! how old are you?

Younger Yute
DON'T WATCH THAT

Reena	i just got manhandled by a yr8 with a growth spurt why is he so tall? / oh my daze
Tia	told u not to back dat drink
Debz	no one even noticed
Reena	i did – my lips did / yukkkkkk
Debz	he was blocking half ur body
Tia	u thought he was cute?
Reena	noO! i didn't . . . but . . . is three years a big gap?

Tia/Tolu/Debz
          YES!!!

Tia   ya tu fassss

Reena   look yeahh, it's criminal to be dat tall! //
          so deceiving . . .

Tia   um hm

Tolu   there's Adam!

Debz   where?

                              Debz *searches*

Tia   slow down!

                    Tia *and* **Tolu** *follow*
              Reena*'s thoughts are magnified*

Reena   . . . *'it's only one life yu get'*
          why do boys get to kiss gyal and keep it moving?
          get a pat on the back and keep it cruising?
          but gyal? we get the verbal bruising! hm!
          forget dat!
          dats why i love my aunty! my aunty?
          she's . . . everything! when aunty's around?
          there's always laughter, stories and fooood!
          when aunty dances and everyone dances
          i get to hear nuff stories about my parents
          all the tingz dey try keep secret!
          my aunty says the truth always sets yu free
          h'even when ya nah lyke di sound of it!
          my aunty doesn't walk with her head down
          my aunty says *'head high and bank account plenty!'*
          she told me that *'people judge, an' if yu 'av a flower
          dem ah go judge yu more'*

          we'd talk vaginas in *code* so my dad
          wouldn't have a heart attack
          she said, people will try to make ur flower define u
          some will even try to

'shame your flower into submission' but!
'yu cyan't let people tek yu for eediat'
she told me a secret one time . . .
my aunty said . . .
dat my flower is a portal between heaven and
earth
and only i hold the key!
true superhero shit!
imma bad gyal!
aunty says
　　'yu haffi run di flower,
　　don't let di flower run yu!!'
my aunty . . .

Tolu　　Reena! u gud?

Debz　　what's wrong?

Reena　　nothin

Tolu　　who do i need to bang?

Tia　　who we fighting?

Debz　　no one

Reena　　i'm just hungry

Tia　　for man?

Reena　　when i'm ready to go in yh,
　　　　　no one better tell me to hold back

Debz/Tia/Tolu
　　　　　oooooo! *(mock scared)*

Tolu　　at least it's finally lit
　　　　　before we stepped in
　　　　　hoodies lined up the walls like a field of corn
　　　　　it was pack out yet the dance floor

Debz　　living room corner

Tolu   was empty
            so we had to set pace

Tia   some of us a bit too much

Reena   well well wellll
            t'anks to me doing teewww much
            Debz caught her very own Jon B!?

Suspense

            did she not?

Suspense

Debz   i did

Suspense

Tia   *you!?!!?!?*

Everything changes.
Debz *and* **Reena** *morph 90s American sitcom style*
part double act and in all seriousness
theme tune soundbite plays

Debz   In her eyes she saw nothing but Gotham
            before her
            A cold winter storm raged as her blood beamed
            with soils of lament

Theme warps/mangles

Reena   Will loneliness comfort me forever?
            DI butters friend would I always be?

Debz   No one to call home

Reena   No orange to her soda

Debz   Home alone like Kevin every Christmas

Reena   Alone like Tracy Beaker on visitation days

Debz   Feigning in the dark like Helga

Reena   Alas

They morph again

Debz   A glimmer on my soul

Reena   Who lives there?

Debz   Hope!

Reena   She finally has her Leonardo Romeo

Debz   My Mighty Ducks Charlie?

Reena   the Pacey to her CREEKS!

Debz   The Duncan to my BLUES!?
The one who will save my bells like Zack! –

Tia   i will bell your head!

Canned sitcom laughter

Reena *halts it with her voice*

Reena   come out my ting man!

PORTAL FLASH

Tia   Can i just say how much i luuuvvvd The Queen's
Nose
Oo Grange Hill! The Bill n of course we were
blessed with the Real McCoy n Desmonds!
but there wasn't much . . .
We only got 2 seasons with Cleopatra!
But with Nickelodeon? N den wen Trouble TV
dropped!!!? Woiii spoilt for choice!
Finally had more shows were we could relate
to in a way, even though it was American
Trapped in the Closet had the endz in a choke hold
n Reena made us watch Dairy of a Mad Black
Woman over and over again!
Looking back it always felt we didn't have our own
British black ting but now i guess . . . we were
part of some kind of . . . evolution?
We were part of making it!

Reena   *ah wah dis!?*
come out my ting man!

Tolu   doing praise and worship for a why'ite boy una?!

Debz   hey! / that's not nice

Tia   some any Sunset Beach ting

Reena   don't HATE.
COZ iiiii! di matchmaker did that!

Debz   and, and do you not have why'ite Jesus hanging
above ur room door? / /

Tia   hypocrisy!

Reena   she does

Tolu   uno how my mum stays though

Debz   and i don't judge yu for dat

Tia   okkk but did you give him ur number?

Debz   i . . . gave him my bb pin

Tolu   skeeen!

Tia   ah yu dat!? / gwarn, Debz!

Reena   AND! Adam's boy who saw me in the talent show
last year recognised me and called me by my
character's NAME
do *you* remember what that was? / /

Tia   no?

Debz   Dionne?!

Reena   dest-tin-nee / ANDDD

Tolu   wawu

Reena   thanks to me a certain someone's crew /
stepped to us and yoooou got to meet **Niel**

Debz   oooo

BROWN TIMS – EVISU JEANS – WHITE T – GOLD
CHAIN – **AVIREX JACKET** – NEW ERA CAP

Tia   Mase's dimples and Kano's eyes
jawline like Romeo from So Solid
wid the cheekbones of Fredro Starr
smooth but gritty with it
mid hench like Ginuwine
never needed to over dew-it
i was in love
he wasn't an emcee
he . . . was a rapper

Tolu   allow it, allow it, allow it!

Tia   come out my memories man
everyone emceed but. He. was.
an intellectual rapper like / 2pac

Ree/Debz/Tolu
Tupacccccccccc

Tolu   we knoooo!

Tia   he stepped right up to me
licked his lips like LL and before i knew it
he had me in paradise
. . . my head hit the floor first thou

all   h'embrassment

Tia   knocked me out
i was blinded by the bling which
shone from his sparkling whites

Reena   shone?

Debz   hear dis gyal pls?

Tia   fam!!!

Tolu   his popeye arms raiseddd her up

Debz   and onto thee sofa

Reena   told one of his boys 'go fetch **thee** water'

Tolu   and from that day forward
               they were **locked at thee hipppp**

Reena   none of us could breathe

Tia   *'Terror but you can call me Niel'*

Debz   Niel this

Tolu/Reena
               Niel that

Reena   Niel this

Tolu/Debz
               Niel that

Reena   he was buff thou!

Ree/Tolu/Debz
               righhhtt

                                              Tia *shoves* **Reena**

Tia   wasn't all looks and young games ee-va!

Reena   umm / hmm

Tia   he always supported me
               we'd speak on the house phone every night
               BT had this first hr free ting
               hang up at 55 minutes
               in order to call again type ting

Tolu/Ree/Debz rob dis h'England!

Tia   but during my exams he wud only call me
               two times a week! played no games
               said i needed to study n be smart so i cud juggle
               bein his wife and a scientist.
               He wud always say i completed him like the
               seventh day

Tolu/Ree/Debz
      aww

Tia   Niel said i woz always seeking info, analytical and
      dat
      so i wasn't down at first but den
      i let him tag me Lady 7
      coz true say in numerology
      7 is the number of knowledge
      Niel understood me
      he took me to West End in a black cab
      one time / felt like a tourist in my own city like

Tolu/Ree/Debz
      (*heavy sigh in longing*)
      . . .

   Tia *sings the opening chorus lines from '21 Questions' (50 Cent)*

Tia   it was real
      Xena and Hercules real
      Chuckle Brothers real
      Posh and Becks real
      Mary and Joseph real

Debz   coz not a lot of men can stick by a woman
      pregnant by someone else you know

Tia   right

Tolu   neeks

Tia   our alien egg had twin babies and everything
      one was gold the other one silver
      . . .
      long story short
      postcode wars
      somethin somethin
      and more dumb sh*t
      joint enterprise
      they were using that to take the piss
      he was innocent

Tolu   did a bid

Tia   just three months!?

Reena   got shipped back 2 yard

Tia   he went to live with his dad in New York

Debz   allegedly

Tia   ANYWAY
we stayed connected
via msn chat

Tolu   and she looked after dem alien
babies like it was real

Tol/Ree/Debz
then everything became about the baby Niel

Tolu   baby Niel this

Reena   baby Niel that

Tolu   he was Jamo init?
always tryna breed

Tia   there's more to the Caribbean
than Jamaica UNO!!

Debz   u luv ur island boyz

Tia   and so do you! / and our music and –

Tolu   hold up!

Reena   our food

Tolu   i've only had pattie once! . . . / this week

Tia   u had curry goat the other day!

Debz   she prefers puff puff!!

Reena   she's the only one who does

Tolu   don't try it! you nyam puff
puff all da time Reena!

Debz   yh! and love off Naija boyz //

Tolu   Obi and Fola!

Tia   experimentations!!

Reena   dere my boys / man!

Tolu   lies

Debz   we coming soon // don't worry!

Tia   whoo!? who ah come?

Reena   when? / when!?

Debz   Africa's coming soon!

Tolu   we're here!

> *They cuss each other out*
> *in their mother tongues/accents*

Tolu/Debz
    Yardie!

Reena/Tia
    h'AffRican!
    and don't get it twisted

Tolu/Tia   i can cuss her out

Debz/Reena
    and i cuss her out

Tolu/Tia   but you?
    better not try it

Debz/Tolu
    it's plantain h'and

Reena/Tia
    planTIN wars
    over here
    4 lyfe

Tia   thank you, Reena

Reena   umm hmm

Tia   no seriously

Debz   i love u guys

Reena   ur so moist

PORTAL FLASH

BAGEL KING

Their bags begin to rumble and activate, the portal beams return, gliding through space before landing on them. Leaving their bodies in a shocked state, words fall from their mouths without permission

Time flies by
> *Existing in fast forward*
>> *We don't realise*

You can't fight time
> *Souls on crunch time*
>> *We'd spend time trying re-E-wind*

Mere mortals
> *dodging life's artful judgement*
>> *You can't fight time*

They look to each other, unsure if they've all experienced the same thing.

Tolu *has a feeling she can't shake.*

Tolu	omdz . . . omdz . . . omdz . . . i just had this mad vision?
Reena	vision?
Tolu	NO WORD OF A LIE!
Tia	vision?!
Tolu	NO WORD OF A LIE!
	talk da tingz den?
Tolu	what I'm about to tell youuuu!!!
Debz	BRUH
Tolu	i was on the way to Bagel King
	YH?
Tolu	and . . . and this plate of Indomie kept following me around!

piss off

Tolu   dat hood indomie!

dat good indomieee

Tolu   where it was made with
             'a kettle n ah plate cover' type Indomie!!!
             deezzzz times i just wanted a bagel
             but the tantalising smell of sweet bread?
             oo! had me contemplating between
             coco bread! apple crumble? bun 'n' cheese!?
             but this Indomie *still* wouldn't leave!!
             then all i heard was

             'THERE IS RICE AT HOME'

                                         They all see what **Tolu** *can see*

Tolu   when Supermalt came through
             trying to get my attention
             knocking on the glass!?

             beside it –

Tia   miss saltfish pattie

Debz   jerk chicken wings

Tolu   uncle jollof

Reena   and cod

Tolu   and chips

Debz   and fork

Tia   **allllll** beckoning me to take a bite!

             felt like

Tia   nine night

Tolu   hall parties

Reena   and the pub

had **a link-up**

Tolu	sonic spinning
Debz	sprinting

boomerang

Reena	around my mind
Debz	no word of a lie

all the food I love

Tia	inna di same place
Reena	**aLL** catering to my tongue

Bodies bend and mould
linking together like Transformers

Tolu	**aLL** telling me to take a bite!
Tia	impregnating my taste buds
Debz	mouth FULL with the **EXpecTAtioN**
Tolu	of the swing of this
Reena	blended
Tia	marriage
Debz	mixture
Reena	fusion

SO OF COURSE I –

They take a bite and it's the loudest 'bite' ever,
mouths chewing on overload.
their bodies have an 'allergic' reaction
as the portal dictatorship returns
teleporting them through dance to another realm
to the backdrop of south London slang
words formed into song and beats
with warped sounds of food being eaten, mashed and thrown.

As soon as they arrive, heads drop down into a standing sleep

A HEAVENLY SOUND

I AWAKE

Tolu   soaked in **blackness**?

Debz   **'Endz-ness?'**
was the sign on the door
before it *flung* itself open

Tia   it was tooo **bright** for my eyes
but poetry clicks buzzing in my ear
had me alert

Reena   shook up my soul

Tolu   changed my sight

Debz   a framed – *one* finger pose?!

Reena   a cropped portrait of
an immaculate screw face?!
slit eyebrows
gold tooth!

Tia   perfection!

Tolu   no word a lie!
the 'black nod' walked by?!

Debz   with fufu on his shoulder?!

Reena   afro comb not far behind

Tolu   is that a shea butter fountain?

Tia   and a gliding power fist?!

Debz   it's all the little things . . .

Tolu   then all i could hear was

'DIS IS DAT!'

all i could hear was

'DIS IS DAT'

Tolu this gigantic **ice cream container** appeared?!
lid lifting an snapping with attitude
with DAT meat from the *stew pot?*
peaking
leaning out
looks me dead in the face
and said

Ice Cream Container
YOU'RE NOT MEANT TO BE HERE?

I'm. not. / meant to be –

Ice Cream Container
YOU'RE NOT ABOUT DIS RIGHT HERE

Not about / whattt? –

Their bodies are propelled forward

Words appear

You – don't know – what you have – so – we – will

Ice Cream Container
SHOW YOUUU

K.O.
[MORTAL KOMBAT]

*Jaws lunge to the side
the punch activates the portal*

*A warped mashup of
'H'enjoyment! – Injectttt it! – Reload it!' can be heard
through the gateways shifting!*

*For the first time their bodies embrace the portal's infiltration,
transforming and transporting as they form
cultural steps and grooves.*

An explosion of rhythm, social dances and freedom.
An appreciation for this cultural integration and power
they had all along but couldn't see.

'I CAN SEE IT NOW' 'CAN YOU SEE IT?' 'I CAN SEE IT!'

THIS IS THAT

A sweet dream. Arriving with true knowledge of self the BBQs hold it down.

Tia	**THIS IS THAT!**
	LENNOX JAB
Tolu	THAT MOMENT BEFORE THE CYPHER
Reena	THAT U GOT 2B BOLD U GOT 2B WISER [DES'REE]
Debz	**DAT** BIG BEN
Tia	DAT BIG BRO **DAT** NU FLOW
Tolu	THAT DMX!
	'WHAT' [DMX]
Reena	THAT BROWN STEW CHICKEN
Tia	**DAT** BROWN STEW CHICKEN BONEEEEEEEE
Debz	THAT
	'SHAAATTAAPPP'
Tolu	THIS IS THAT AUNTY SHOLA'S *GÉLÉ* DOING '*OSHEY BADDEST*'
Tia	IT'S THAT ROLLING LAUGHTER
Reena	**DAT** SPRINTING LAUGHTER
Tia	**DAT** SCATTER
	AND 'SHUT THE FUCK UP'
	I'M THROWING A SHOE
	TYPE LAUGHTER

Debz	**THIS IS DAT** H'AMM GONNA LOOOOSEEEEE IT **THAT**
Tolu	OFF HER WIG
Reena	DAT TOOTHBRUSH

SLAYED **SLICKED**

SWIRL **EDGES**

TO DA GODS!

SNATCHEDDD!!

PERIDOT.

Tia	**IT'S DAT** ROLL DEEP AVENUE
Debz	IT'S THAT ACCOLADES UPON ACCOLADES
Tolu	IT'S DAT SIDE OF THE ROAD PEPPERED WELL STREET SUYA
Debz	IT'S GHANA WHERE OUR COCO BEANS IS MELANIN RICH

Reena	IT'S DAT CHRISTMAS SORREL
	     THAT CROP OVER SUGAR CANE
	     THAT RUM WHEN
	     THE MOON IS HIGH
	          WATER IS MELLOW
	          AND THE SKIN
	          IS GLISS-EN-IN

Tia	DAT **'GAZA FOREVER'**[2] DAT GOOD AS FI DEMMMM!!!!! **GYAL GOOD AS FI DEMMMM!!**
Debz	IT'S WHEN YOUR MOUTH CARRIES SOUNDS OF EXPRESSION THAT WORDS JUST CAN'T REACH

---

[2] Cultural slogan from Vybz Kartel

'AHH'   'KAI'   'REEEEEY'   'WOIIIIIII'

'AHH'   'REEEEEY'   'KAI'   'WOIIIIIII'

'AHH'   'KAI'   'REEEEEY'   'WOIIIIIII'

Tolu   MELODIES SO SWEET LIKE THE YORUBA
              TONGUE

              THIS IS DAT

Tia   RHYTHMS BOUNCING ACROSS THE WALL
              SNATCHING YOU UP ON SUNDAY
              MORNINGS

              DAT

Reena *sings words from 90s garage tune.*

              DAT

Tolu *spits epic bar from grime riddim.*

              DAT

Tia *sings words from 90s RnB tune.*

              THIS IS DAT

Tolu   OOUURR OURRRR [D DOUBLE E]

              DIS DAT

Tia/Reena

              POW YH THAT POW [LETHAL BIZZLE]

              THIS IS DAT

Debz   TUH TUH TUH
              21 - TUH TUH TUH
              [SO SOLID CREW]

              TUH TUH TUH'

THAT
              **'BRUKATAH BRUKATAH –
              MY FAMILY'**

A snippet from 'Touch Ah Button' by Sneakbo disrupts space, they go nuts!

Tolu   THIS . . . IS THAT **HIP HOP**

Reena   THAT FLOETRY

Debz   THAT DEAR MAMA

Tolu   THAT MISSY

                THAT UNBOUND

Reena   DAT GRACE JONES

Tia   **THAT** GENESIS

Tolu   DAT SUNNY ADE

Debz   **DAT** FELA KUTI

Reena   **DAT** BOB MARLEY

Tolu   **DAT** TALKIN' DRUM

Tia   **DAT** STEEL PAN

Reena   DANCE BURSTING THROUGH OUR SKIN

Debz   INTO FESTIVALS OF EXPRESSION

Tia/Reena
                NOTTING HILL COULD NEVER

                CONTAIN WE

Tolu/Debz
                CONTAIN **SHEEE**

                NO WORD OF A LIE

hot breaths, heavy sweat, and weighted silence they acknowledge how far they've come. a mixture of spoken words singing and black church affirmations repeated to infinity:

This is That ... Black Love

THIS IS THAT

LOVE

THIS IS THAT

THIS IS THAT

Blackity blackity black
Blackity blackity black
Blackity blackity black

LOVEE

THIS IS THAT!

No Word Of A Lie
No Word Of A Lie

This is for my people

THIS IS FOR THE PEOPLE

This is . . . Love

Before I Go

For the mandem, 'famdem' and westside of London.

'Mandem'

A collective noun for a bunch of boys or men,
particularly your own group of mates.

Characters

Ajani (AJ), *twenty-one, male*
Messenger
Marcel, *twenty-six, male*
Mummy, *fifty-four, female*
Reeks, *twenty-one, male*
Nicole, *twenty-one, female*
Rene, *twenty, female*
Mandem

The play runs with live musicians. The musicians are metaphorical extensions of **Ajani***: the drum his heartbeat, the sax his heart strings, etc. . . .*

Act One

On stage we see an electric barbecue, bottles of alcohol and –

Ajani *(twenty-one) – a boisterous and charming young man who jams with the live band of musicians, getting gassed in preparation for his event.*

As the audience file in **Ajani** *welcomes them, occasionally flirting with random people.*

When the doors close, **Ajani** *turns on his speaker.*

We hear his phone via Bluetooth.

Bluetooth Voice   The bluetooth device is ready to pai–

The bluetooth device is connected uh successfully.

Ajani *confronts the audience. Excited to welcome his guests.*

Ajani   Welcome to AJ's BB –

Bluetooth Voice   Call from mandem.

Ajani   Oh shit. One sec!

He goes inside and checks his phone. He goes to answer but then backs off. Hesitant. He watches it ring out. A voicemail from **Mandem** *plays.*

Mandem   This guy, why don't you ever pick up your phone? F1 just told me what happened last month. What?! I couldn't believe it, bro. This is what I'm saying, that could have been it. Again, it's the same shit. Yute's dying in the ends for stupidness. You need to be careful, bro. I don't even know how to say this but . . . If you died, fam . . . Like if it was a different situation . . . I don't even know, man . . . just – just move correct. Yeah? Call me back when you get this.

Bluetooth Voice   Press one if you'd like to save this message. Press two if you'd like to delete this mes–

Ajani *taps.*

Bluetooth Voice   Message deleted.

9th Wonder, 'LoveKills!!!' plays.

Ajani *is clearly affected by the message but brushes it off. He notices wires around the BBQ. He plugs it in.*

Next, he grabs a bottle, opens it and starts to record a Snapchat video.

Ajani   Ay listen! You already know the vibes, BBQ is ready. I've got a free yard and we're 'bout to pack this shit up! Keep on inviting your friends, it's 'bout to be a movie!

He flips the camera to himself and takes a few swigs for the camera. After he stops recording he coughs.

Ajani *(watching the snap play back)*   Come on . . .!

He scrolls through other Snapchat stories – we hear them from the Bluetooth speaker. He stops on a particular snap. It sounds like a group of girls getting ready. One of them is **Nicole**, *his ex-girlfriend.*

Snapchat Video *(Ice Spice – 'Munch' is playing. The video is a collection of girls talking over each other, dancing and bantering)*   You thought i wuz feeelin you!!!? . . . Naaaa, uh UH, go on with your bad self! . . . Nooo! . . . You bad bitch! Ahhhh!

Ajani *darkens. This one is harder to brush off. He replays the snap. As he re-watches, he takes a big swig of the alcohol. It plays over and over until –*

Bluetooth Voice   Call from Reeks.

Ajani *lets it ring out. We hear a message come through.*

Reeks *(in a car)*   AJ, my darg! I'm gonna be late but the mandem are gonna get there soon! You don't know them but they're cool.

This annoys **Ajani**.

Reeks   Also, bro! Have you seen Rene's snap?! I think I seen your ex in her snap. Is she coming? *(Laughing.)* The

fuck?! . . . Also, bro, save me chicken I beg. Alright, love –
love.

Ajani *takes a swig then replies.*

Ajani   Reeks, my guy, Ay listen I just realised there are
wires on your BBQ. Are they electric? . . . And did you invite
them road yutes? How can they be my mandem if I don't
know them. I thought I warned you about chilling with –

He deletes the message.

(*Trying to be light.*) Reeks, my guy, I beg you come quick to
operate your electric grills . . . and Rene? Fuck Rene, bro. I
don't even follow none of ex's friends anymore. Bun them
and bun her.

He deletes the message.

(*Trying to be light.*) Reeks, my guy, who the fuck buys an
electric grill – come and pattern your machine. And, Rene's
snap? Yeah I seen it. I saw Nicole in it. Nicole is nuts, bro.
She can come if she wants, I don't even care . . . I'm out
here, living my best life. Feeling all summer summer
controlla –

*He deletes the message and throws his phone on the table. He finishes
the last of his vodka and stares quizzically at the electric grill. He
goes to touch it until 'knock knock' – he checks his watch.*

Oh yeah!

*He drops to the floor and does various worksouts before taking off his
top and wrapping it across his shoulder.*

Then he opens the door.

A slow beat comes in. **Ajani** *performs to the audience. He flows with
the beat.*

Ajani
    Welcome to AJ's BBQ,
    For those of you who don't know,
    This is the greatest event of the year,

A place where all the yutes can meet and feel no fear
A place where all the gyaldem reach to vibe freely with
their peers
Yes, welcome to AJ's jamboree
Once you step foot in this house, you're a part of my
family.
At AJ's BBQ we don't discriminate,
If your vibe is magnetic,
There is space to accommodate.
This BBQ is soaked in ancient history,
This BBQ has rules that need to be followed according
It's not just some shubs,
Or some house party
AJ's BBQ is tradition, that needs to be nurtured carefully.
You see,
All this quality is contained whilst filling up your tummy,
I swear AJ's BBQ gives carnival a run for its money.
So before you slowly trickle in ima need you to pay
attention.
These rules are important to me and are needed to run
the function.

The beat gets a little faster.

Ajani
No one go upstairs. Apart from the mandem.
If you jump on the aux, turn them notifications off.
If you want to do up DJ, make sure the tunes are jumpy
Eat until your belly is full, but make sure your feet still can
move.
If house music starts to play, abandon all activities and cut
them shapes.

The beat speeds up into a house beat. He dances.

Ajani   At 5pm sharp we hold a silence for Grenfell. Their
families are forever in our hearts.

*He stops. After a silence he sips his drink and pours the rest on the
floor.*

From inside, his phone rings interrupting.

Bluetooth Voice   Call from 0112 3304 –

Ajani   Shit. One sec! Yeah I know, rule number two!
One sec!

Ajani's *rushes to his phone and answers.*

Police Voicemail   At 5pm. This call is from a person
currently in prison in England/Wales. All calls are logged
and recorded and may be listened to by a member of prison
staff. If you do not wish to accept this call, please hang up
now.

Ajani *leaves his phone on the table on loudspeaker.*

Marcel   Hello? AJ?

Ajani   Yes, bro! What you saying, Marcel!

Marcel   You know, same old. Missing you lots.

Ajani *stays quiet.*

Marcel   It's the 18th fam. You doing the BBQ?

Ajani   Of course! This is the most important day of the year!

Marcel   Yes . . . Where's Mum?

Ajani   Got a free yard. She's working as always.

Marcel *(sighs)*   She okay?

A beat.

Ajani   She's still running around, kicking. Put her in the
right colours you'd think she's Drogba.

Marcel   Did you talk to her about it?

Ajani   The time will come. There's time for everything.

Marcel   Until time runs out.

Ajani *stays quiet.*

Marcel   Don't let Mummy work herself to death. Are you going to do it soon?

Ajani *stays quiet.*

Marcel   Talk to me, bro.

Ajani   I'm talking, fam, I'll do it.

Beat.

Marcel   Anyway I'll leave you to the BBQ . . . Make sure it's mad you know? Don't disappoint me.

Ajani   I'll catch extra whines for you.

Marcel   I love you, bro. I miss you.

Ajani *stays quiet.*

Marcel   Alright, love.

The phone cuts. The music remains off. **Ajani** *grabs a slightly bigger bottle of brandy. He drinks. Then drinks some more. He goes to touch the grill until – 'knock knock'.*

Ajani   My guests!

He goes back to the audience. Getting more and more drunk. **Ajani** *heckles the audience.*

Ajani (*this can be improvised*)
Ohh shit it's looking full out here!
Yes yes, you man. You good? Nice puffer jacket, bro. And pouch that wraps it all up . . . You must be Reek's boys. Are you not hot?

Anyway you've come just in time for my last rule.
No lurking on the wall.
I want everyone dancing, vbzing and catching whines
And I'm talking tekky whines
Like whines that push you off balance whines
Whines that's circulate you with too much velocity whines
Grab a bredrin 'cah your falling whine,
whine

Whine till you feel it your spine
Till she can feel it in her behin–
Ye
But you keep it respectful . . . yeah I'm looking at you.
With your two strand twist and your magnum bottle.
to make sure you man have no excuse
Watch closely, I'ma show you.

He demonstrates.

The way to approach a whining goddess is simple,
If you can't get the eye contact before, then you touch
gentle
Before you make total contact It's essential,
That you wait and pay attention for the look back of truth.

'She' screws up her face.

In situations like that
Take the L and fall back
But if it's like this

'She' smiles back gleefully.

Then move with confidence and twists your hips.

He dances with himself.

YES! Don't hold back, my people, let it all out and have fun!

AJ Tracey's 'Bringing It Back' plays. **Ajani** *drunkenly backs off and admires his creation. Until 'knock knock' –*

Ajani *goes to the door.*

Rene (*a mixture of different female voices too*)   Yoo, AJ! Open up!

Ajani   Fuck that's Rene!

He starts panicking. 'Bringing It Back' winds and contorts with a mixture of 'LoveKills!!!' spilling in.

What the fuck?

He slaps the speaker but nothing happens.

(*Addressing the audience.*) Ay! Who's hungry? You man want chicken?

He runs over to his last bottle of Wray and Nephew and downs half of it. He rushes over to the grill.

Yeah! I'm a bad boy chef you know!

The knocking on the door has turned into banging.

Let me put some flavours on this thing!

He pours the Wray and Nephew into the grill and walks away. Smoke slowly starts to emit.

There's a saying in my ends! You can run but you can't hide from uncle Wray's. This shit will take you out!

Rene   AJ! Open up, man!

Ajani *ignores the door, getting more and more worked up.*

Ajani   You man want drinks?

He runs and gives out bottles of alcohol to his guests.

Rene   Ajani!

Ajani   The food might be done . . .! Who wants smoky BBQ chicken!

He opens the grill and it explodes. **Ajani***'s scream is cut short. A fatal blow. He drops to the ground dead and the stage darkens and fills completely with smoke.*

Act Two

The stage transforms and we are in a gloomy afterlife. It's dark and smokey. The instruments glow with a ghoulish light. We can only see **Ajani***'s silhouette. He manages to stand but can't move freely.*

We start to hear fragments of his consciousness. We hear glimpses of what is yet to come: voices from the people **Ajani** *holds closest.* **Mummy**, **Marcel**, **Reeks**, **Nicole**, **Mandem** *and* **Messenger**. *All sounding disjointed and unclear.*

Ajani's Consciousness (*voiceover*)
    The world is closing in on me.
    Illusions, sights, all surrounding me.
    My heart's beating fast, uncontrollably.
    My mind begging for peace, tranquility.
    But it doesn't come. It grows worse. A curse.
    A tear in my consciousness.
    Fear bringing tears to my eyes.
    My soul reaching unwanted quietness.
    Move . . . MOVE!

Voices   Ajani, my boy . . . Our future's that our decision . . . You're stiff . . . I still remember that day . . . Mandem . . . my hours . . . Time runs out . . .

Ajani *is being overwhelmed by his mind. Suddenly it stops. A blinding light surrounds him. He stands in limbo. Completely baffled.*

Ajani   Hello? . . .

After a long beat.

Where the fu–?

Messenger   Language.

Ajani *jumps.*

Ajani   Who's that?!

Messenger   I'll be your host.

Ajani *looks for the voice.*

Ajani   Where are you? Come out, fam!

Messenger   I'm everywhere.

Ajani   Yoo . . . are you God?

Messenger   No, not God. Think of me as a messenger.

Ajani   Messenger?

Messenger   You're in limbo. The afterlife.

A beat.

Ajani   The afterlife! Are you saying I'm dead?

No response.

I can't be dead! No way . . .

Messenger   If I had a penny for the amount of times I've heard that.

Ajani   If you're not God then what are you?

Messenger   Just someone who passes on the message.

Ajani   So what, are you some send-out for God?

Messenger   Don't be silly.

Ajani   Does God send you shops, yes or no?

Messenger   Okay, goodbye.

Ajani   Wait! Sorry, I'm joking! This is just a bit mad, you get me?

Messenger   Ajani, I've been expecting you. I had no idea you'd be like this.

Ajani   What do you mean expecting me? What are you like Death then?

Messenger   No.

Ajani   You've been waiting for me to die? That's kinda fucked up . . .

Messenger   A few months ago you barely escaped death. If you remember. We nearly met.

Ajani *remembers.*

Ajani   This is weird, fam. I don't feel dead . . . Have you got the power to get me out of here?

Messenger   No.

Ajani *freezes in disbelief.*

Messenger   But you do.

Ajani   What does that mean?

Messenger   If you can learn to communicate you can pass on.

Ajani   Are you saying all I have to do is ask?

Messenger   No.

Ajani   Then what the fuck are you talking about.

Messenger   Language!

Ajani   I don't understand.

Messenger (*sigh*)   Ajani, you've spent a large part of your life avoiding your emotions. Like many men before you, you can talk, but you can't 'communicate'. As a result, you've shackled your soul. Until you learn how to 'communicate' and free the burden, you won't be able to leave this place.

A beat.

Ajani   I beg you stop chatting shi–

Messenger   Hey –

Ajani   This isn't some joke, fam! I can't be dead! I got shit to do! I need to get back to my BBQ!

Messenger   Here we go.

Ajani   You're mocking it! You trying to say I don't know how to talk? If there's anything I can do, it's talk! I've spent my whole life talking! I fucking love talking! Are you listening?!

Messenger   Shouting at me with 'foul language' isn't going to help you. Have you thought about communicating with me?

Ajani   You're gonna get me mad!

Messenger   Try to communicate with yourself. Explain that to me. How do you feel?

Ajani   If you're bad, come out here right now! COME!

Messenger   So you're angry, Ajani?

Ajani   Yeah, I'm fuming!

Messenger   There's a start. Why?

Ajani   Because you're taking man for a dickhead. I told you already I need to get back! I got things to do! There are people that need me.

Messenger   Like who?

A beat.

Ajani   My – my peoples innit. My family.

Messenger   Family? Your mum?

Ajani   I meant my peoples!

Messenger   What about your brother? If you was given one last chance to talk to your family what would you say?

Ajani *is caught out – his emotions are getting the best out of him. He's struggling to contain them like he normally can.*

Ajani   Dont talk about my family – you don't know me!

Messenger   I know you feel guilty. Don't you?

Ajani *doesn't respond.*

Messenger   You feel like it's your fault. You're the reason their happiness is limited. You're nothing but a burden.

Ajani   No!

Messenger   Are you scared, Ajani? Are you sad? If your mum was here what would you say?

Ajani   Nothing! I have nothing to say to her, fam!

He paces in discomfort . . . unable to hold himself back. Muttering to himself.

Messenger   Just speak your mind. Let it spew out of you. Don't hold back. Let your thoughts out. Dont deny them, accept them. Let it out. LET IT OUT. NOW! AJANI!

Ajani   IT'S LIKE SHE STEPPED OUT OF HER SKIN SO I COULD GO IN. IT'S LIKE SHE STEPPED OUT OF HER SKIN SO I COULD GO IN. ITS LIKE YOU STEPPED OUT OF YOUR SKIN SO I COULD GO IN.
Transfused your blood without my permission.
I didn't want it. That juice isn't worth the squeeze.
Don't jeopardise your life for me.
I want you to be free . . . away from all the fuckeries I want you to be happy and go out there and chase your dreams.
How can I be sane knowing you did it for me? What kind of sick fuck can sleep peacefully knowing selfishly my family reduced the quality of their life for me.
You say it's not as bad as I claim it but let's face it. It's facts.
You had to do certain things so I could relax.
That's tapped, fucking aggravating, clapped.
My mind, I'm not even sad . . . I'm mad!
I can't live from the labour of your shell! Your hard shell ripped off your skin. Shell so soft, it's kind. Kind of a pillow.
I scream into you releasing stress but also thankful I have a place to rest my head. In the safety of your comfort.
Can I be that for you? Can the roles switch and you be fulfilled from my pain. I'll work, I won't complain

I'll do it all again and again until you're safe. I'll sacrifice parts of me to re-create the things you lost. If I could give you years of my life, instantly I'll stop the clock. Would you let me? How can I repay you? Can you set my soul free?

I'll make you happy. Mark my words, your greatest desires will watch you with envy. Your dreams and aspirations will gossip consistently, wishing they could have a taste of your new found serenity. I'll make it happen, your essence will shine. All the hardships will slowly wash away. Waves of pain will calmly evaporate. You'll be rinsed from sin forgiven once again.

A blinding light pierces through. **Ajani** *stares out to the light.*

Mummy   Ajani Adeyemi. My son. Thank you for speaking to me. I didn't know you felt this way. I only work hard because I want you to have the brightest future. I understand how you feel and I'll cut down my hours. Let's spend more time together. I love you. My boy.

Ajani *takes in his mother's words. A weight off his shoulders. The blinding light goes.*

Ajani *is silent.*

Messenger   'I have nothing to say to her, fam.'

Ajani *keeps quiet. He's speechless by his outbreak.*

Messenger   How did that feel?

Ajani   Different.

Messenger   You've been talking – a lot, all your life but this was the first time you communicated.

Ajani   Yeah.

Beat.

Why?

Messenger   A number of reasons. It's a suppression that has been passed down from generations. Societal and cultural.

Ajani   Why does everyone always make it about race?

Messenger   Don't be silly, I'm making it about you. A man. A black man.

Beat.

Why haven't you spoken to your mother?

Ajani   Because I wouldn't want to worry her. I wouldn't want her to think I'm stressed out. Or weak . . . But that's because she's fragile. Life's been hard on her. It has nothing to do with being a black man.

Messenger   Black men have felt the need to single-handedly sustain their household for generations. Years of systemic racism and patriarchy has built a box around the black man and told him he cannot be weak. No human is built to carry the weight of the world. Even your neck gets tired from carrying your head.

Beat.

Ajani   Raa. It did feel good though! It just came out of me. I feel different now, fucking hell.

Messenger   Hey! –

Ajani   My bad bro! I'm just gassed. But isn't swearing a form of expression?

Messenger   It's lazy. There is power in your words. Choose them wisely.

Ajani   Raa. But admit it was mad.

Messenger   It was alright –

Ajani   Why you hating, bro? I was talking from an inner conscience . . . My body feels . . .

He rubs his body. Something has changed.

Actually my body doesn't feel too good. It's harder
to move.

Messenger   Oh yeah, your time here is at the expense of
your body. In the real world time has significantly slowed
down. Right now your physical body is still technically alive.
However, if you don't learn to 'communicate' in good time,
your body will die and you'll remain here *forever*.

Ajani   Fuc– Damn.

He takes it in.

So can't I go back now? Haven't I learnt to 'communicate'?

Messenger   Ha. That was just a glimpse. You have a way
with words but that's not enough.

A notebook and pen fall from the sky.

Your gifts are your words. Write something – what you just
done was free-form poetry. You should try different forms of
expression.

Ajani *picks up the book.*

Ajani   This seems long, bro – how do I do that?

Messenger   By communicating.

Ajani   This again.

Messenger   There are people in your life who you need to
speak to. Communicate with them.

Ajani   And as soon as I do that, I'll go back to my BBQ?

Messenger   Only if you're truthful. Also, you're stiff – don't
neglect your body.

Ajani   Who you calling stiff, bro –

He twists his hips.

Messenger   That's clearly all you know. Communicate with your body first, then communicate through it.

Ajani   What, which one do I do first?

Messenger   Look, I'm tired of speaking. My mouth's dry, I'm going.

Ajani   Tired? I thought you was omnipotent?

Messenger   I told you I'm not God.

Ajani   Oh yeah, send-out.

Messenger   Bye.

Ajani   Wait! I was joking . . . ! What do you mean bodily communication? Like dancing and that?! Man don't dance, fam.

Silence. The **Messenger** *is gone.* **Ajani** *looks around.*

Ajani   Oi, send-out? Come back, bro . . .

He explores limbo. Eventually, he starts to write. Time passes. He makes progress – we think he's on the ball then he screws up the paper, chucks it and starts again. This time it looks like he's making good progress. He laughs to himself . . .

Ayy, messenger,

A slow beat comes in.

not gonna lie you told me to write this speech or whatever but . . . I don't know who to write it for or where to start. I don't know who to pick. Not gonna lie, for most of my life, I've been a shit.
Not gonna lie, I often put myself in sticky situations
Not gonna lie, I often end up wronging a lot of my people dem.
To be fair,
To be completely honest,
Most of my offences are technically biased,
Like, it is subjective to be offended,

What you choose to let offend you is technically up to you.
However, for the sake of my decaying body,
I've written this piece to say sorry . . .

Boss man at West Nine Food and Wine.
I apologise for wasting your time,
That time you clocked the Supermalt in jacket.
And I tried to say when I walked I already had it.
We argued for about ten minutes . . .
Not gonna lie. I lied.

Postman P,
I heard you banging on my door to deliver my deliveries,
You was out there in the cold, rain pouring down endlessly
But not gonna lie, I aired you to get more sleep.

Tina my neighbour,
You're always there for me in when I need a favour,
You see your cat that gone missing? The one on the poster?
Not gonna lie, I saw the cat scraping a fox and I couldn't be
arsed to save her.

Uhh, Nicole. My ex,
Actually, bun that . . .

Uncle that drives the 316 bus.
I told you I got brutally robbed and had no means of going
home.
I told you it was an emergency, that you had to let me on.
You said you'd get in trouble if you had done that. But you
did because I reminded you of your son, Ameka . . .
Not gonna lie, I haven't seen you driving the bus in time, I
hope you're good and that . . .

Miss Hazel,
Man like benny,
Lucinda, Jayda, Stacey.
Fats, Stabber, Tanika
Lincoln, Maya, Stevey
You man all borrowed me money.

Not gonna lie, you'll get that when I come back.
And lastly,

Lastly, messenger, I'm sorry for calling you a send-out.
That's out of order, I'm sure your position of work is very
important and senior.
But not gonna lie,
That's not gonna stop.

He strikes a pose.

Yoo, messenger, what you saying? Was that lit? Was that
good like?

A blinding light pierces through. **Ajani** *looks to it.*

Messenger (*dramatically*)   Ajani . . .

(*Back to normal.*) Yeah, that wasn't it.

The lights go back to normal.

Yeah, very funny, but not gonna lie –

Ajani   Ay!

Messenger   You better get serious.

Ajani   You told me to communicate with the people I owe
na?!

Messenger   Yes, but not about a £1.29 malt beverage.

Ajani *laughs.*

Messenger   Do you want to get back to your BBQ or not?

Ajani   I get you but I can't get it out. It's like I know there's
something but I don't know what.

He is uncomfortable and stiff.

Messenger   Walk into the centre.

Ajani   What?

Messenger   It's okay. Just trust me.

Ajani *walks into the centre.*

Messenger   Take a deep breath. Then exhale.

Ajani *does as instructed.*

Messenger   Take two steps to the left. Two steps to the right. Good, good. Take two steps back. Take one step forward. Take one step back. Take one step forward, then turn around. Then start it all over again.

Ajani *does as instructed.*

Messenger *hums the 'Candy' melody*

Ajani *realises* **Messenger** *is messing with him.*

Ajani   Are you taking the piss, fam!

Messenger   Yeah, you're stiff.

Ajani   Ahh, you're a dickhead!

Messenger   Your body and your emotions work together you know?

Ajani   Don't ever do that again, fam.

Messenger   When you're scared, you tremble. When you're angry, your heart beats faster. When you're hungry, your belly rumbles. When you're horny, your peni–

Ajani   Eee, I get it, bro.

Messenger   Earlier you said 'man don't dance' – why doesn't man dance?

Ajani   Because I'm a bad man. Man don't dance, fam. I cut shapes at the raves and I catch whines at the shubs, but you'll never catch me doing up contemporary. I get you want me to express myself but the mandem don't do that, you get?

Messenger *(getting angry)*   If you want to put yourself in a box. Then you can also remain in this box until your body corrodes.

Ajani   Allow it.

Messenger   Why are different types of bodily expression excluded from the 'mandem'? Movement is important. It's a bridge between the physical and spiritual. I've existed for a long time and movement has kept its importance. It's a medium to converse with your ancestry. Don't you want things to change? You need to grow up. To be able to communicate *through* your body you must first communicate *with* your body.

Ajani *is taken aback by* **Messenger**'s *mini-outburst.*

Ajani   Okay, bro. But that doesn't change the point. Man don't dance, I don't know how to do them things.

His body is weighing him down.

And I'm running out of time. I can feel it.

Messenger *takes a breath. Regaining composure.*

Messenger   Where can you feel it?

Ajani   All over, fam, like –

Messenger   Be specific.

Ajani *tries to tune in.*

Ajani   Around my arms. My shoulders. Yeah my shoulders.

Messenger   Take a breath and focus it into your arms. Try to imagine your arms are breathing.

Ajani   Don't mess me about you know.

Messenger *chuckles.* **Ajani** *does as such. He closes his eyes.*

Messenger   Now move your body the way it wants to. What else feels stiff? What else needs to be relieved?

Ajani *moves his body expressively and feels it.*

The movement felt refreshing. He does it again. He looks around self-consciously.

He begins to express himself physically. At first he's not sure what to do. He begins to connect and starts to explores his different emotions. A tribal communication with his heartbeat.

It works! He runs to his notepad and writes things down.

Act Three

Ajani Ay, Messenger, you was right. Again. That was fun, fam. Felt like I was in a playground, like my body had a mind of its own. Moving and fixing itself. My back was clicking and all sorts . . . as I was doing it, I had this mad thought. Imagine if all the mandem in ends linked up in the park and just done that! It would look so random, but equally beautiful. A sea of working-class bodies ebbing and flowing amongst each other. Feeding each other's energies.

He starts moving again.

Sway to the right and see man like Leon handing out KAs.

He sways the other way.

Retract back and see Linda bussing joke with the young Gs.

He stops.

We don't do that enough you know. It's like everyone's out there for themselves. The ends has so much to offer but instead it does nothing but take. I've realised how much we are influenced by our community. Marcel is in jail because he loved his family and our community.

He looks at his notepad.

You see Marcel yeah, he's the best guy. He doesn't swear like me, you'd love him. Everyone loved Marcel. He's that guy in ends that you cross the road to spud. He treats everyone with so much love. He got arrested doing an armed robbery. At the time my mum was struggling and my young stupid self wasn't helping by always asking for the latest BlackBerry. Back in '15 Marcel tried to rob a money deposit box. He got caught, pleaded guilty and took the rap for the mandem. Back in '15, I learnt a valuable lesson.

Beat.

A beat comes in.

Ajani
November 21st, back in '15
Was the worst day for me to fuck around in history.
Miss Firefly kept me back at the end of the day.
And I was just sat there angry squeezing a ketchup sachet.
But that day, something was off
Because no matter how hard I squeezed the packet
the ting didn't pop.
My grip weren't soft.
I've always had a heavy touch
But I was feeling weak that day
Like my powers had been sucked
I was feeling mad in school that day.
Like I was angry in school that day.
Some brudda in the year above violated Nicole, my girl,
earlier today
and I told him buck me after school
But I also got detention,
So now I'm sat here feeling like a fool.
You see Miss Firefly yeah? Sometimes she can be a right
bitch . . .
Na I'm chatting shit, she's mad cool. I'm just feeling mad
pissed!
As the clock ticks I'm just there squeezing the shit out of
the red packet.
But it's still not popping –
Like I'm putting full power
Not just scrunching
But twisting
Pulsing
Folding
And it's still not fucking popping!
The bell rings.
It's time to go! Grab my tings and speed walk through the
corridor
I buss through the door
Expecting to get straight to scraping
But there's no one. Not even a few of the mandem.

Just an empty parking lot
I mean of course not.
It's fucking five o'clock.
So I start bopping home.
I dash the ketchup.
Right now,
If anyone acts up
I swear down there gonna get touched.

Ajani's Consciousness (*voiceover*)

It's like I felt empty, hollow inside
It's like I had no energy,
No power resides
I was feeling weak
No strength inside of me
I wasn't ready for those words
I think you've broken me.

Ajani

So now I'm near my street, and I'm dragging my feet
I've messaged everyone in the group chat and they've all
left me on read
They must think I'm a neek
They must think I'm afraid of the streets
I know that brudda was a road man
But I've never been scared of defeat . . .
I reach my front door and then I double text Nicole.
She's ain't replying like usual like she ain't feeling man no
more.
I put the key in my door and I get a chilling vibe, I don't
even get why
But it felt warmer outside
I walk up the stairs and I hear some heavy breathing.
It's either someone's laughing or crying but it's giving me
this weird feeling
It's my mum
she's sitting there alone in the dark
she's struggling to breathe because she's been crying so

hard
She's wailing
and gasping
It's making man feel uncomfortable
I ask her, Mummy what's wrong? She's looking really
vulnerable
I make her take a breath, (breathe)
Mummy what's going on?
She looks at me and says, Your brother,
his life is done
They gave him life sentence. Called him a dangerous
criminal
He's just my baby boy, he just hanged with the wrong
people.'
Then she starts again it's like she can't breathe.
It's a horrible sight to witness
Your mother on her knees.
The sound is so haunting, I can hear her soul screaming.
I don't move an inch, I'm just stuck watching frozen.
I just watch it
my eyes dry
my body has no motion.
My heart is breaking every second but I'm holding back
the emotions
I need to be strong for her
I'm not gonna cry with her
I'm the only man left in this family
I'm gonna provide for her
I'll be that guy who can fix it,
Ill be that guy who built it
I'll be that guy who is strong and big
I'll be that guy who is perfect.
I stand there for an hour and watch her cry herself to
sleep.
I drop my school bag at the front door and head back
onto the streets.

Ajani's Consciousness (*voiceover*)

It's like I felt empty, hollow inside
It's like I had no energy,
No power resides
I was feeling weak
No strength inside of me
I wasn't ready for those words
I think you've broken me.

Ajani

The way I'm bopping is different now like my mind's
feeling distant now
It's like I want to cry but my body feeling stiffer now.
Nicole sends me a message.
It says, can you come over to talk real quick?
The timing is real shit but I might need this. I might need
Nicole to fill up my spirits
Nicole gets me proper.
Me and Nicole were raised in the slumbers,
On the blocks us two were trouble, but the tolls weren't
always equal.
The things I did to get respect were different to the things
she had.
If she had done things I thought I had to do the ends
would call her a slag.
It's fucked up logic that I didn't understand.
Until I fell for her
and seen the effects first hand.
I throw a stone at her window and she lets me in.
As soon as I see her my body warms up from within.
She says, where have you been?
I say I was stuck in detention
She says you left me by myself
I say I didn't mean for that to happen.
But something has happened.
And as I'm trying to speak, I feel something's coming over
me.
Like I can't control it. It's taking a hold over me.
Nicole sees me struggling to get out my words

and uses that opportunity to get out hers.
She says
'That brudda violated me today
And you did nothing
You let them treat me like a clown everyone was laughing
After school I waited, I thought you was coming
They kept calling you a pussy and it got me to thinking
. . .'
But as she's talking my body starts shaking. My face is
warming up and my heart's really hurting.
She says
'Why didn't you bunk detention?
Why were you standing in the back?
When that brudda called me a slag why didn't you
instantly scrap?
I need a man in my life who got me.
I need a man in my life who I can trust to always be there
to protect me.
AJ. I think you're weak.'
Naa this is peak.
I adjust my feet from side to side.
I look her in the eye.
Then I start to cry.
Like really cry.
Like I'm biting my lip crying
Like I can't breathe crying.
Kinda like my mother's crying.
Nicole turns away like she can't bear to watch
She speaks to me softly and finishes the job.
'Ajani, that's enough. I can't be with a boy.
I need a man. I'm sorry. It's over.'

Ajani *struggles to say the words of his consciousness. But he does.*

It's like I felt empty, hollow inside
It's like I had no energy,
No power resides
I was feeling weak
No strength inside of me

I wasn't ready for those words
I think you've broken me.
Back in '15, November 21st, that was the last day I cried.

He sits in silence. A blinding light pierces through. **Ajani** *looks to it.*

Marcel   Ajani, I hear you, bro. I'm sorry for compromising the family. I know my absence put heavy pressure on all of you. I wish I could have done things differently but it's too late for that. The past can't be rewritten but our futures are our decision.

Ajani *is meditating on* **Marcel**'s *words. His world is becoming peaceful.*

Messenger   Ajani, how you feeling?

Ajani   Good. I don't think I can move much. My body is decaying faster than ever.

Messenger   You've come a long way. You're close.

Ajani   I think I'm nearly ready.

Messenger   Yes, you've been communicating well, you have completed the first step. But still need to go further. You need to confront the people you've been avoiding . . . Only after then, your soul will be set free. Do you have anyone in mind?

Ajani   Yeah, I think so.

A silence.

Messenger   Cheer up. Your BBQ awaits . . .

Ajani   Thank you.

Silence.

You gave me gift. So thank you.

Messenger   Don't be so soft. I'm joking. I'm playing. Kidding around.

Ajani You good?

Messenger Yeah, yeah.

Ajani Talk to me.

Messenger (*a small laugh*)   It's just normally you guys are just happy to pass on. No one has ever thanked me.

Ajani You meet a lot of us?

Messenger Yeah. There's a lot of young boys still being forced to grow up too fast. Patriarchy and absent male figures leaving gaps in young men's socialisation . . . It's tragic. Hopeless.

Ajani But you've helped me. Men like you who are there to guide, inspire and help the ones who get it wrong will bring change.

Messenger I've been here for years. When will it change?

Ajani You're bugging. It's not all going to happen instantly, as long as today is brighter than yesterday then that's your job done.

Messenger *takes it in.*

Messenger Ajani – one who overcomes the struggle. Your words are your gift. Use it for good.

Ajani *writes in his book. He adds finishing touches.*

Ajani Messenger, what's your real name? Who are you?

Messenger I am Messenger. Your voice, your matter, your thoughts. I am you.

Ajani   . . . I prefer send-out.

He gets up and starts to hum a soft melody.

(*Sings.*) Ohhh, ohhh, ohhh, ohhh.

The English language is flawed.
Some thoughts can't be described with words.

Some feelings haven't got appropriate verbs.
There's no actual definition for the term love.
I don't know what I'm tryna say but I'm tryna say
something.
I'm stuck in between denial and acceptance.
My heart is neither complete nor tattered. Not broken. Not
damaged. Not void. Not vanquished. Not there. Not
present.

Lost.

(*Sings.*) Nicole where did you go . . .

Look at me singing tunes.
Look, I'm tryna reach you.
Look how I'm vulnerable.

(*Sings.*) Where did we go wrong

Believe it or not, I've run out of words.
To express what I feel inside I need sounds.

(*Sings.*)
    Ohhh, ohhh, ohhh, ohhh?
    Nicole, where did you go?
    Where did we go wrong,
    I searched up high and
    I searched down low?
    Nicole, I need you to come home.
    Nicole, where did you go?
    Come back to me, I won't run no more.
    Nicole, why's it been so long?
    I forgive you for all your wrongs.

Ajani *belts the melody until he can't anymore. He squeezes out his
last breath. A blinding light pierces through.*

Nicole   Ajani, I still remember that day. November 21st.
The day you came to my house and cried. The day you came
to me for support and I pushed you away. I watched you
change into a different man. I watched you grow further
away from who you are. Instead of apologising for the

damage I knew I done, I projected. Ever since that day we lost our love. I'm sorry, Ajani. I won't hide anymore. Even if we can't be lovers, let's be friends. Thank you, Ajani.

Ajani *raises his arms triumphantly and waits.*

And waits . . .

But nothing. The light dims away. Nothing has happened – he's still in limbo.

Ajani   Argh!

He is so weak it hurts. He nearly crumbles but he holds himself up. He's fading away.

Ajani   Messenger?! It didn't work! I'm still here!

Messenger *doesn't reply.* **Ajani** *is about to fade away until –*

Ajani
Not yet . . . I defy death until my final breath.
I defied death, I'll defy it again.

He pulls himself together. He reaches for his book, opens it and prepares himself for his final words.

Ay, mandem! Are dem man der really your mandem?
My bruddas, my mates, my guys,
my sisters, my wife. Mrs Firefly . . .
To that cool cousin at family events . . .
That blessed co-worker on twelve hour shifts
Your dog that reminds you every day you're missed
The mandem. That there is the mandem
The mans there that make you feel whole. Held even. See
you on road spud you, transfer the blessings.
Like, when I'm feeling down negative
my knuckles needs a charge positive
to spark up my engines. Fuel me up for the day.
'Tell mumzie I said hey!' Ay!
The mandem! God bless the mandem!
Even when eyes link in unfamiliar territories
there no worries

A head nod or a tap to the chest signals the alliance
In a moment we share a common ground on cracked
concrete.
The mandem
All been through trials of life but still see you and choose
to side with the light, even though there's darkness. Failed
relationships and misplaced love. Leaving us broken.
Seeking for release in dangerous places. This journey
repeated for many generations.
I see it
Especially in my own folk who feel the need to get
involved in criminalities . . .
Tryna provide for me and my family, but in the process
shedding their skin.
Loving so hard they give their hearts in.
It's mad because they only feel the need to provide
because society has found a way to divide us man
from certain opportunities and lifestyles from other kin
man der.
Other kin with next skin man der. Who am I kidding man
it's unfair.
Systemic racism. The oppression and collection of
working-class black brethren placed in under-developed
locations with half-hearted educations and a system that
tells you you can't win.
But the mandem are kings. We innately feel a need to
uphold and provide. So we start chilling with bare
different guys and make it by any means –
the mandem.
Sometimes turn gang them but it's just the search for
family.
It sometimes unfortunately spirals into acts of vanity
but the source is a direct response
of poverty.
Man.
Den the media kicks off and the mandem is a dark image.
Because black is evil right?
The shadow of night sneaking up in white Britain. Doing

all the killings. Even though we built the buildings and
healed the fallen that's because we're British. Not black.
But the mandem see they forget all of that. They live
happily and banter daily.
There's certain man I see and I feel healed. I feel grateful.
It brings tears to my eyes I'm thankful. Because a lot of
you don't even realise how much you've done to impact
my life. When I was young and thought being the
mandem was all about a life of sin and gang violence, you
man slapped me up, kept me straight, showed me that the
life you lived wasn't all that great. It was a sacrifice for kids
like me to elevate. How I can not feel happy cause –
when I got stabbed last year
all you man rid for me. I was angry,
I protested
I wanted to come.
Why you man putting your life and freedom on the line
for something so dumb? It's my problem yeah? Let me
solve it!
But what you man said was

Mandem   'Ajani, just make it out the hood.'

Ajani
and you went there instead. I was happy to hear you
didn't even take revenge you just got me an apology. That
made me really happy.
My mandem. Fam dem. From the west side of London.
Touch the roads down on carni, yeah we're all
baccanlaning,
From the trenches we emerging.
So we standing, shouting! Upholding our young kin.
Reminding them every day we are all kings. We work
twice as hard but it's calm. We have the capacity. Our
mouths can drink gallons, nothing can silence me. So
when I see you man chilling the park. You know I'm
gonna scream,
Ayy, mandem!

'Cah I'm gassed! The love you lot shown me, I'm sending it right back.

A blinding light floods in. **Ajani** *looks to it.*

Reeks   My broksi! Bro, you got me gassed! The mandem! I hear you.

A mixture of different male voices emerge. It's the **Mandem**. *The echo of voices from the different generations of men fuse and compile.*

Mandem   Thank you for sharing / I hear you, bro / My guy / Love my brother / Thank you for sharing . . .

Ajani *listens. He takes them in. Proud. The voices quieten until –*

Messenger   You don't need to defy death. Define it.

Ajani *holds his chest. He understands. He is covered in a mist of smoke. He begins to fade away. To his true death. He doesn't fight it, he is content.*

Suddenly, the BBQ lights up. Just as **Ajani** *is about to fade away we hear –*

Nicole/Reeks/Voices (*inaudible at first. Then slowly building up*)   AJ? Ajani! Give him space. AJ! Wake up!

Nicole   Ajani? AJ!

Ajani *turns his head towards the BBQ.*

Cut to black.

The End.